Also by Chuks I. Ndukwe
Available everywhere

The Courage To Aspire
A MATTER OF FAITH

What Reviewers Wrote About
"THE AUDACITY OF DESTINY"

"...Ndukwe's spirited storytelling makes the book worthwhile."

—Kirkus Reviews

"His writing is fluid, using slang and casual speech as well as some technical jargon. He employs both humor and pathos as he frankly describes his fortunes and misfortunes. His destiny has indeed proven to be audacious, as he illustrates with such incidents as being unexpectedly gifted a new car by a concerned neighbor and securing a loan for his first home purchase after doing what came naturally to him—kindly assisting a lame stranger trying to crawl up a set of steps. The stranger turned out to be the realtor he had come to consult. These and other striking occurrences have brought Ndukwe to the conclusion that "there's goodness in every soul waiting to be awakened." He also acknowledges that he has often been the recipient of "American generosity." Today he is "happily retired" in New Jersey and has resolved to use his writing talents and his unique understanding of life's surprises as a means to help others. RECOMMENDED."

—The US Reviews

"A true survivor. I believe this book will appeal to readers interested in a comprehensive and motivational life account of someone who endured hardships and overcame them."

—OnlineBookClub Reviews

"This story of his life journey has a specific purpose beyond chronicling events: to chart the progression and evolution of *"...the awesome Irresistible inner-power or the inner-guide we all have inside of us."* This translates to a survey that nicely juxtaposes personal experience with broader inspections of life purpose, blending philosophical and spiritual insights into a bigger picture.

The Audacity of Destiny a compelling autobiographical exploration of the roots and realities of achievement, destiny, and motivation."

—The Midwest Reviews

"This book is all about the journey. It helps you recognize the magic moments that jumpstart our journeys in pursuit of our destiny. Author Chuks Ndukwe takes us on his story with him, narrating the intense lows he encounters like war, the death of loved ones, getting laid off, and more, while sharing the highs that keep him moving forward. It teaches us that while we are never prepared for our journeys, we should be ready when the magic moment arrives. Because if we are, we can achieve some truly amazing things like Ndukwe did. And trust me, he does some truly amazing things in this story.

The author has a particular skill in short lyrical phrases that help us better understand our situations and the lives around us. He shares insightful moments with the reader as well as influential opinions on topics like being a good engineer, a good teacher, or even just a good person. But perhaps my favorite aspect of this book is Ndukwe's nuanced view on destiny. He sheds light on the way that we see ourselves and on our perpetual search for whatever we expect our lives to become. There are quite a few parts in this book that felt refreshing and original, and I'm so glad they were included.

The Audacity of Destiny definitely has something to offer its readers. It is a great example of succeeding through perseverance for all those who are ready to take their next step. It is a first-hand account of losing battles but continuing on despite the pain in pursuit of their journey. This inspirational memoir could help you open your eyes and prepare you for your destiny—if you're up to the challenge."

—Independent Book Reviews

We have addressed each reviewer's editorial issues in the final round of editing and made reading this book an enjoyable experience.

THE AUDACITY OF DESTINY

Thoughts On Life When The Irresistible Inner-Power Leads The Way.

Chuks I. Ndukwe

THE AUDACITY OF DESTINY: Thoughts On Life When The Inner-Power Leads The Way.
Copyright © 2017 by Chuks I. Ndukwe
All Rights Reserved.
Published in the United States of America by Ikebiebooks in association with Ingram Spark. Distributed by Ingram

The Library of Congress has catalogued both the paperback and ebook editions of this work as follows:

Publisher's Cataloging-In-Publication Data
(Prepared by The Donohue Group, Inc.)

Names: Ndukwe, Chuks I., 1942-
Title: The audacity of destiny: Thoughts On Life When The Inner-Power Leads The Way / Chuks I. Ndukwe.
Description: [Newark, New Jersey] : Ikebiebooks, [2018]
Identifiers: ISBN 9780999070505 (paperback) | ISBN 0999070509 (paperback) | ISBN 9780999070529 (ebook) | ISBN 0999070525 (ebook)
Subjects: LCSH: Ndukwe, Chuks I., 1942- | Resilience (Personality trait) | Self-actualization (Psychology) | Fate and fatalism. | Consciousness.
Classification: LCC BF698.35.R47 N38 2018 (print) | LCC BF698.35.R47 (ebook) | DDC 155.24--dc23

info@ikebiebooks.com
855-336-7770
Library of Congress Control Number: 2018901294
ISBN 13: 978-0-9990705-0-5 (Trade Paperback)
ISBN 10: 0-9990705-0-5

Dedication

To those who embrace obstacle as a stepping stone and failure as an opportunity for a fresh beginning. And to others who see failure as a signal to change course.

Contents

Epigraph xii
Preface xiii
   Chapter 1 1
Heritage and Character 1
      Character Formation 2
   Chapter 2 10
Essential Preparations 10
      Let the Child Play 11
   Chapter 3 20
Magic Moment 20
      Instantaneous Reaction 21
   Chapter 4 33
The Inner-guide 33
      Screaming Inner Voices 34
   Chapter 5 43
Mother's Advice 43
      Teaching Moment 44
   Chapter 6 61
Choice and Option 61
      The Power of Choice 62
   Chapter 7 74
Mending Broken Spirits 74
      Cultivating Respect 75
   Chapter 8 85

The Journey	85
Beyond The Shores	86
Chapter 9	92
I Became Me Here	92
Learning and Practice	93
Chapter 10	108
Being A Scientist	108
Job Lends Credence	109
Chapter 11	117
Pride and Rivalry	117
Order and Logic	118
Chapter 12	127
All Set To Go	127
Stepping Out	128
Chapter 13	142
The Grand Finale	142
Laudable	143
Chapter 14	152
Marriage and Family	152
Shattered Lives and Faith	153
Chapter 15	167
Helping Hands Abound	167
Good Deeds	168
Chapter 16	175
The Monkey Wrench	175
I Am Crushed	176
Chapter 17	186

The Ultimate Goal	186
Destiny	187
Epilogue	192
Acknowledgements	196
About The Author	197
Other Books	198

Epigraph

✳✳✳

Destiny is preordained. But not in the same manner as death. In the case of death, we don't work to find it—it's omnipresent and ready to grab us at any time. Whereas destiny, although similarly ubiquitous but hidden from common knowledge, catches nobody. It's each life's sacred mission, the discovery of which fulfils its meaning and purpose. So as I see it, destiny is our reason for being and for which we are remembered long after we depart the earth. In essence, it is our footprint on the sand of time. For one who leaves without a trace is one whose existence is forgotten soon after he departs.

Preface

It is not in the stars to hold our destiny but in ourselves.
~ William Shakespeare

Most parents tell their children, *"You can achieve whatever you put your mind to,"* like they're destined to do great things—even if it's something entirely absurd. What a load of utter crap! It's like telling a child he can fly, without actually explaining that the only way he can do so is by an airplane or some other airborne object. A wise man said this once:

> **Show a child something to think about instead of how to think. Because every breath-taking magic event is likely to capture his imagination and get him off the street.**

Destiny and hope serve different purposes in our lives, but there is one thing that they share in common—each is deeply rooted in its mythology that often bewilders the human mind. While the word hope is a desire or wishes with the belief that you can obtain what you hoped for, destiny is said to be the foreordained future we're fated. The mystery of destiny resides in its deity and a man's fantasy that one day, the god or goddess will bless him with the goal he seeks in life.

Very often, you hear celebrities—movie stars, music stars, comedians, and various other performers spit false attribution of their performances to their destinies as though destiny and achievement are the very incarnations each other.

For years, I tortured myself questioning the integrity of the notion of destiny. I asked myself questions like: How come only the successful invoke the word? What about the people who never make it out of their neighborhoods, and end up on the street; is that their destiny? Why should a precious child whose success came from inheritance utter the

THE AUDACITY OF DESTINY

word destiny with the same breath as a poor kid who amid insurmountable social and economic odds makes it to where even the wealthiest struggle to be? That's my quibble against destiny—the concept seems to belong to the affluent, but then I take comfort in the definition I found in my dictionary:

'Continuing activity and functional behavior that tend to determine final status, especially as to progress or decadence.'

Marcus, my church pastor, once spent his whole sermon on destiny, describing it as a predetermined end of the journey of life. I've got to be honest; throughout the speech, I rightfully felt like he was talking about death, because let's face it, that's the ultimate end to the journey of life.

So I ask; don't we have to make some necessary preparations to start a meaningful journey? What if one fails to prepare for this journey, what happens then?—Silly Questions, right? Whenever I hear someone say: life is a journey, the same silly questions light up in my mind and then I ponder upon my own experience and the journey it has been. How is your journey? Can you recall how you prepared for your life's journey? When did it begin and what kind of ride has it been so far? Do you remember all the left and right turns and all of its ups and downs? You don't—it's impossible to remember every single detail.

Yes, I agree journey is an apt metaphor for life that begins right from the day we're born. It reminds me of a baby who sits up for the first time, claps and giggles proudly—the befitting acknowledgement of that very first achievement of his life. Later on, the same baby begins his regular, incremental, and successive performances such as crawling, speaking, walking, and running until that "I'm a big kid now," declaration. The big kid starts school—his first formal venture into the real world, interacting with other kids, acquiring social skills, discipline, and intellectual development. Around eighteen, the big kid graduates from high school and becomes a young adult.

At this moment, one can safely assume the child is fully prepared for the rest of the journey, and that's what we believe. However, is he ready for real? If so, well then he's all set for whatever life throws at him. However, if not, what happens next? Please allow me to remind you of an indisputable fact we tend to overlook—the choices a child makes at this juncture may determine the course and tenor of his remaining life's journey.

What I am implying is that a child who plunges into the workforce straight from high school may find his journey more challenging than his friend who underwent vocational training and even more difficult than his other friend who went to college.

However, regardless of the choice and direction he takes, it is possible for the journey—his life—to end on the point he never dreamed of reaching. One of the advantages of living an exhaustively active long life is that you have the time to take stock of your experiences—where you've been, what you've seen, and done, and the ensuing results of it all. Plus, you realize that there's something present in your life that made your journey possible. It's called "human interiority complex" (the Irresistible inner-power, non-carnal senses, conscience, and the inner-voice). These four elements of life exist in contingent symbiosis to navigate the journey along the guard-rails of natural order to a point where we can say "yes, this is my destiny."

Let me simplify the concept and call it the awesome Irresistible inner-power or the inner-guide we all have inside of us, and that is what I wish to write about through my own life experiences. This book goes beyond the narrative of one man's journey and teaches the reader valuable lessons.

It aims at clearing the blurred perception of destiny and provides a unique window into the mechanics of the human interiority complex from within which the inner-power drives the journey of life. It simplifies the concept of destiny with the following humanizing metaphor.

The appropriate metaphor for this inner-guide is your daunting but loving guardian. This powerful guardian takes you places; think of an amusement park where you're enjoying the rides and having the time of your life—until the guardian yanks you off the ride and takes you to a place he thinks is best for you. This place is not necessarily the one where you'd like to be, but that's where you end up. The guardian

THE AUDACITY OF DESTINY

senses danger and takes you away from it too. He allows you to make mistakes and suffer the consequences of it. He keeps putting you through this painful experience until you find something fun and safe that you love and can enjoy with your friends and then he leaves you alone for good.

Similarly, once you successfully invoke your inner-power to lead your life, you will find yourself in different situations where you're inspired to reach new heights and others where all you get is pain, suffering, and agony. So that's how you know that we're in pursuit of elusive truth that transcends our understanding of where and how to find it. It's a monumental task—giant puzzle each life is assigned to solve at creation. Although we can say in many different words and in so many ways that we hold our destiny in ourselves, yet it is when and only when our inner-guide matches the work we do on earth to our reason for being—our purpose in life that we can honestly say that "this is our destiny."

In the end, it's an indisputable truth that a poverty-stricken child from the remotest part of the world has equal right as the richest and most powerful man on earth to the pursuit of his reason for being.

Finally, it is the mysterious ways our inner-power in concert with our quest for destiny overcomes all obstacles along the way that anchors the title of this book: *The Audacity of Destiny*.

Chapter 1

THE AUDACITY OF DESTINY

Heritage and Character

My heritage has been my grounding, and it has brought me peace.

~Maureen O'Hara

THE AUDACITY OF DESTINY

Character Formation

Education has, for its objective the formation of character.

~Hubert Spencer

Far, far away from the hustle and bustle of the city life exists a small village in the hinterlands of the eastern region of Nigeria where children rolled around in the sandy playground. Birds chirp and hop about on the orange trees, and dogs play the game of "catch me if you can" with the cats.

From the north, you descend into the valley that gradually ascends to the first village— Amigwu. Past that village, you go downhill once again into another valley that gradates into the village of Amoji. From there, you travel along the level plains for a while until you find yourself in the heart of the famous farmers' market (Eke). That's where you begin another climb to the square of the last village—Obuchie that silently sits atop the hills overlooking the villages you just passed through.

The town of Alayi comprises of two sections separated by a highway. My part is called Amankalu, and the other part is called Akoliufu and sprawls out there like a distant world from us. The Alayians are ridiculously proud people—so incredible that they nicknamed their town, Igbojiakuru (the preeminent producer of a unique brand of yam the Ibos are known for). I am not kidding, that's how proud they are—obviously the notion of which their neighbors hold in trivial objection.

There's something peculiar about Amigwu; it's bounded on all sides by elevations with trees towering into the sky. Around the playground, called the square, mighty orange trees stretch their branches wide enough to shelter kids from the sun. They sit there emotionless, with steadfast patience and nondiscriminatory indifference, as kids frolicked around them, hugged them, climbed them, and sat on their branches to eat their ripe fruits without yelling or kicking.

Boys played soccer games with vigor—in the evenings, on the market days, and Sundays. These boys did not play soccer for money or scholarships or fame. They just played for the joy of it, and that was enough; in fact, more than enough for them. Girls played games too. They held hands and moved in a circle and the opposite direction. They played a game where they faced each other, slapped each other's palms, crossed hands, and repeated the sequence with captivating speed. They jumped ropes with both legs, one leg, and stooped down to touch the ground before standing back up again on their feet. Just like the boys, they too played with vigor just for fun and joy of being able to indulge in an experience like that.

The girls' games interested me more for obvious reasons— my cousin, Egbichi was one of the girls playing alongside the other girls while the boys played soccer. We loved to cheer each other no matter what game he or she played. It just came naturally to us; it had been that way since the day we were born—the same day, at the same time only minutes apart. So we cheered, supported, and protected each other from what, I'm not sure, even now as I write about it. Sometimes I wonder how different my life would have turned out if she were not there.

People walked everywhere. They walked on stones, gravel, sand, and mud depending on the weather and wherever they went, they went barefoot. Uncle Okereke Chima lived a few miles away from our village, by the Methodist Church. So, I walked back and forth from our home to his delivering messages from Dad and vice versa. Visiting him always gave me an extra surge of energy. Believe it or not, I ran most of the way to his house, even with the blisters on my achy, bare feet.

My dad had two nephews, Uncle Okereke and Uncle Emeke. He

THE AUDACITY OF DESTINY

loved them dearly and was exuberantly proud of both of them. In his mind, they were the smartest people in the world. I could not blame him knowing in his mind; the world was only as broad and expansive as Alayi.

We had no cars, Lorries, buses, or motorcycles running around Amigwu. There was nothing to disturb my village's serenity, except when the Methodist reverend visited in his car. On each occasion, we would gather around his car and pretend like we were pushing it. Then the priest would join us in the act and drive slowly until the vehicle descended the steep slope and sped away. Then we'd cheer, wave, and the reverend would wave back. Honestly, life was that simple.

Villagers worked in the farms seven days at a stretch and rested on the eighth day—the Eke market day—in essence, the calendar week. The calendar year for Alayi started in September and ended in August. Although not defined as such, the New Year was in essence, the New Yam festival, which marked the beginning of the yam harvest season with colorful entertainments and displays. At night when the festivities ended and darkness set, families would gather around to watch the year depart and usher in the new one. Children afraid of the mysterious New Year, stayed close to their parents—in my case, my mom because Dad was always at the square banging "Ikoro" the historic wooden hollow-log loudly to signal the departure of waning and arrival of the new year.

A loud explosion-like sound would sound from far away and got closer and intimated the neighboring villages to get in the action. In the end, Amigwu would finally pick up the noisy clamor, bidding the year good-bye and imploring it to take all their problems, aches and pains, and sicknesses with it. The partying and dancing would continue all night after that.

There was just one tiny regret—the flames from burning wicks women made from palm oil would not burn all night. That essentially meant the party had to end when the fire burned off. At dawn after the celebration, you can't help but wonder, *"Wow! What a beautiful place to be born in."* I was proud to call Amigwu my home and Alayi my birthplace. That's my heritage, that's where I was born.

Chuks I. Ndukwe

My cousin Egbichi and I did not seek school out, the school found us. The Methodist Church had decided to start an elementary school in Amankalu—the part of Alayi town where we lived. Most kids of school age attended the Methodist Central School, so the number of children left to start school at the church was fewer than required. My uncle was the preacher at the church and a friend of the man chosen to start this school.

Every Sunday—after church service, Uncle Okereke Chima, Azik Ukachukwu, Okorie Elendu, and that man visited my dad, and he entertained them with palm wine while Mom served a delicious meal. Egbichi and I were almost four and not quite ready for school then.

One Sunday afternoon, I was riding on Egbichi's back when Uncles Okereke, Azik, and the stranger walked into our house. Dusting off the sand to go in and greet the visitors, Dad called me. Egbichi went home, and then I went inside the house. Uncle Okereke stood up, took my right hand, put it over my head and asked me to touch my left ear. I tried and couldn't even reach close to it. The stranger and Azik tried too and failed. They had me at it until I began to feel pain in my neck. Suddenly, they said together, *"Yes, he touched it."*

At that moment, Dad wanted to know what the reason for the hand-twisting-neck-breaking exercise. Then Uncle Okereke told Dad they needed me to make up the number of students required to start school.

"He's not ready for school yet," Dad said as he brought out a jar of palm wine.

"He'll just be making up the number," the stranger explained.

Mom served her Sunday meal amidst all this discussion. When they finished eating, I ran to Egbichi's house and told her I would be starting school at my uncle's church. Mama Anya, Egbichi's mom, heard what I said, left the house, and came back with a smile on her face. *"Egbichi you are going to school with Ogbuleke,"* she said.

We were ecstatic. Typical I must say, we hugged each other,

screaming and jumping in joy until both of us fell to the ground. Then we got up and went back inside the house—beaming. So, there we were, registered for school without dressing up and heading to the school to join the never-ending line for registration.

During all this time, Mom's stomach had gotten big, so every time she was in a good mood, she'd tell me she had a baby in her tummy. Then after several months of telling me to feel the baby in her stomach, I woke up one morning to women singing and dancing in our house's compound.

"Your mother had a baby this morning," my dad apprised, *"Go and see the baby in the bedroom—his name is Anyele."*

I was afraid at first, wondering how the baby came out of Mom's stomach. However, once I saw her carrying the baby and smiling at me, my fears turned to admiration. I sat beside Mom, shaking the baby's tiny soft hands as the women came in groups to congratulate my mom. My brother was born just about the same time I was about to begin my schooling.

It was a momentous foggy morning—on the day school started. We ate breakfast and then Mom escorted us to the village square where we waited until restlessness set in. Suddenly, a tall woman approached us.

"Mama Nwaka," she called out to Mom.

"*How are you, Jeni?*" Mom greeted her back.

"*Mr. Okpee instructed me to pick these two kids up. I will walk with them back and forth to school every day,*" the woman said.

From that day on, we walked to and from school with the woman named Jeni, behind us. Sometimes she even held our hands on the way. When school began, that stranger who almost ripped off my hand trying to get me to touch my ear introduced himself and the tall woman to the kids; "*My name is Mr. Nnaji Okpee. You can call me Mr. Okpee—and this is Miss Jeni Okorie. You can call her Miss Okorie,*" he told us.

On our first day of school, Mr. Okpee separated the kids into two classes—Egbichi and me too, after the Morning Prayer. Miss Okorie had Egbichi's class, and Mr. Okpee had mine. School turned out to be fun. We learned letters, numbers, songs, and we played a lot too.

Chuks I. Ndukwe

December came with a final examination of everything we had learned during the school year—it lasted just a week, so it wasn't that overwhelming for us.

On the last day of school, we all gathered in the church early in the morning and sang songs led by Miss Okorie. After that, Mr. Okpee called the names of the kids, who passed the examination.

"Those who did not hear their names will repeat elementary one," he said before continuing, *"The first in my class is Ogbuleke Ikebie, and the first in Miss Okorie's class is Egbichi Ejere."*

Then he let us stand on top of his table, and requested everyone, *"Please clap for them."*

The whole school clapped. It was such a moment of pride and achievement for us. Egbichi and I were over the moon. For us, that day was the beginning of the Christmas holidays.

The next Sunday, Uncles Okereke, Azik, my teacher, and Miss Okorie visited Dad as usual. They ate, drank palm wine, hugged Egbichi and me, and congratulated us for coming first in the examination. As we watched Dad and his visitors celebrate loudly, I felt a sense of unyielding self-confidence and possibilities mixed with unquestionable optimism that I'd come first every time I take an examination. It's natural. An unexpected win fueled by the drive to excel, makes you feel invincible—like you're on top of the world—especially when you're a kid. The whole world seems to be just an arm's stretch away for you to grab.

When school reopened after the Christmas holidays, things had changed. Egbichi had left to live with her brother abroad, I was moving on to elementary two, and my teacher now was Miss Okorie. There was nothing left of Egbichi except the memory of both of us standing on the headmaster's table being cheered by other kids in the school. It was a beautiful memory to have, and that alone sent me to a peculiar state of buoyancy, where I kept hoping I'd stand on the table every time the teacher announces examination.

The villagers had built elementary two classrooms during the holidays and equipped it with desks, chairs, and easels. The building

THE AUDACITY OF DESTINY

contained two classes, Miss Okorie's elementary two-A and Mr. Ume's elementary two-B.

Miss Okorie's class was more fun than Mr. Ume's. She taught us the alphabet song, and I sang it everywhere, even at home. School closed again for Christmas holidays in December, and I had this one precocious prescient thought that "I am big enough to play soccer with other kids,"—kids who were much bigger than me. They have been attending the Methodist Central School already which I still wasn't old enough to attend. Understandably, they did not take it well—I got pushed down with sand in the face and ball—smashed on the back; the experience was painful, so I ran back home crying and complaining to my mom.

One day we were returning from church when the rain began to fall, and Miss Okorie did not have an umbrella, so we got thoroughly drenched. When we got back, Mom gave Miss Okorie some dry clothes to change into and washed Miss Okorie's drenched dress and hung it to dry. She looked like a village woman, so I teased her about it.

"What's wrong with that?" she asked, chasing after me. My mother and I shared countless moments like this one throughout my childhood. Later that evening, Miss Okorie went home and then I went out to play at the square.

On another occasion, on our way home from school in the afternoon, Miss Okorie and I stopped at the square to play soccer. I looked around, and there was nobody at the square, so I felt at ease. In case you're wondering why I made sure there was nobody around. It's because boys from the place I came, do not like to be seen playing soccer with a woman, but I'm glad I played with Miss Okorie because she knew how to play. She was surprisingly good at it. So we chased and dribbled the ball around each other until I got tired. Then she picked her books up which signaled the end of the game, so we went home sweating from all the fun play.

To most of you, this account from my childhood may appear quite ordinary. I agree it is on the surface. However, this telling is not published just to give you a window to look through into and see how amazing my journey life has been in the past. It is in fact about the things—important things I learned through these experiences and how they've helped me throughout my life's journey such as the inspiration a child can draw from the parent-teacher happy relationship.

Chapter 2

THE AUDACITY OF DESTINY

Essential Preparations

Tell me and I forget. Show me and I remember. Involve me and I understand.

~ Chinese proverb

Chuks I. Ndukwe

Let the Child Play

Play is the highest form of research

~ Albert Einstein

I love going to school and I'm excited and ready for primary school, but there's just one problem; It's Alayi Methodist Central School, sitting on a high elevation and the road leading to the school? Well, its surface was stones and rocks. I can see the height on which it sits from my village, and the thought of climbing the hill had taunted my young mind. It's a journey I used to look forward to but now hardly welcome. Nevertheless, I got ready for school, wearing my old uniform. Shortly, Dad came home from wine tapping, and then Mom and I left for school.

We arrived at the Methodist Central School, where Mom asked somebody who looked like a teacher, to show her the headmaster's office. He showed Mom where to sit and wait for the headmaster. Then we sat on that long wooden bench under the tree until the headmaster came to us and asked Mom if she was waiting to register her son. *"Yes, he attended Amankalu Methodist School for two years,"* Mom said. *"Well then, he has been registered already,"* the headmaster replied and showed us the standard one (first grade) classroom where a few kids were sitting in the class already waiting for the teacher. The teacher Mr. Igbokwe arrived with the register in his hand, called each kid's name and showed them where to sit. Mom waited until he called my name, then she waved to me and went home. I sat in my seat alone, although I was surrounded by other kids—apart because I did not know them and did not feel their presence. "Don't worry, you are safe in the classroom as always," I told myself to dispel my anxiety. I believe it's the best

THE AUDACITY OF DESTINY

advice—perhaps the only one a child could give himself.

The school held two separate assemblies. Every morning and afternoon, standards one through three assembled in one hall, and grades four through six gathered in another. Boys and girls shared everything except sports and restrooms. We had fewer girls in the class because villagers valued boys' education more than girls. We spent the morning session getting to know each other followed by lunch after which school closed, and kids ran out of the classroom eager to get home. I felt awful; I was on my own and Mom had not told me what to do when the school closed nor how to get back. I was just about to cry when an older boy from my village, Ugoji Kanu called out to me, *"Ogbuleke, school is over. Let's go home!"* I picked up my lunch box and followed him. On reaching home, I saw Mom was standing in front of our house, anxiously waiting. *"Thank you, son, for looking out for Ogbuleke,"* Mom said to Ugoji. *"I forgot to tell him how to get home after school."*

After that horrific experience, I went to and from school with Ugoji and other village kids. By Monday, I had my new school uniforms sewn and went to school looking spick and span. Mr. Igbokwe's brother, Christian, was in my class. After a few weeks, we clicked and became good friends. During manual labor, Mr. Igbokwe would send us home together to clean his house. Sometimes, he'd come home and prepare food for us and then we'd eat and wait for the closing bell to ring before we'd run back to the class and join the other kids.

Mr. Igbokwe came from the adjacent town and loved to spend weekends at home with his family. The teachers' residence and the village seemed like two different worlds on weekends and after school—one deserted and quiet as a ghost town and the other bustling with kids playing in the square. Each time Mr. Igbokwe went home, he'd seek permission from Mom and Dad so that I could spend the weekend with Chris. And we'd run around the school and ate fresh guava, and mangoes.

We took our final exams in December, and I got my first experience of the happy-times at the end of the school year—happy days. Teachers spent two weeks grading the tests. Like birds let loose from the cage, kids ran wild in the bush, picking fruits and playing hide and seek. We went to the motor park, Ozara Desert, Ezialayi Valley, and beyond. Meanwhile, graduating seniors came to school in any clothes they wanted while others still wore the school uniform. On the final day of school, kids who failed the examination cried all the way home, while those who passed, comforted them. It's the school ritual one witness after exams.

A Dove in The Teacher's Hand

Can you recall anything unusual about your relationships with your teachers growing up? Did you know you had one, and how did you feel about it? For me, though, I can recall everything about each teacher I had—inviting me to spend weekends with their relatives at the teachers' residence, our interactions in the classroom, visiting my parents and taking me home to spend holidays with their families. I think about it now and wonder:

> **Why did every teacher I had had treat me like a young dove the keeper takes out of the nest to teach it how to fly and brings it back safely?**

The school year began, on a brisk, sunny Monday morning. My classmates and I sat in the class with the repeating-students chatting about the Christmas holidays. Suddenly, a tall, bubbly, beautiful, light-skinned lady, Miss Neka Azubike walked in, stood in front of her desk, and called the roll. The first time I met Miss Azubike's sister, Erika, I'd gone inside Miss Azubike's kitchen to remove the ash in the cooking-place, and Erika was collecting firewood to cook breakfast. *"Do you like doing this every morning?"* she asked. I nodded and left quickly before Miss Azubike came out.

Getting home, I could not play with my brother that day because he had a fever and I did not go outside to play either thinking he'd get worse if I went out to play. But Mom insisted I go out and play, so I went out and joined the other kids at the square. Now, all the kids were talking about their teachers—the good ones and the not-so-good ones,

THE AUDACITY OF DESTINY

but Miss Azubike was a new teacher, and nobody knew anything about her. At dinner, Dad asked about school. *"Pay attention to your teacher,"* he advised and repeated a million times.

On Easter Sunday, Miss Okorie came by, and she and I went to church together. We sat on the pew listening to the choir. Then she said quietly into my ears, *"Look who's coming to church."* I turned around and saw Miss Azubike, Mr. Mbakwe, and another woman entering the church. They walked in and sat beside us. Miss Azubike sat next to me as I sat still—shy of sitting between my past and present teachers. I was unable to move or say anything out of shyness. I stood up when they did, sat when they sat and looked straight without turning my head.

Usually, Miss Okorie would give me some money for offering, but that day I wasn't sure she'd give me any money. As the offering tray moved closer, I felt like walking out of the church, but without a word, Miss Okorie put money in my right hand, and Miss Azubike put cash in my left hand. It was a bit awkward. Finally, the tray reached us, and then I dumped the money in the offering tray with both hands. It felt like only yesterday I was in Miss Okorie's class, but sixteen months had passed, and she was still going to church holding my hand. Honestly, I felt suffocated by three ladies—Miss Okorie, Miss Azubike, and Mrs. Azubike.

On our way home, Miss Azubike introduced Miss Okorie and me to her mother. *"He's a nice little boy,"* Mrs. Azubike said and grabbed my hand immediately as we walked home, while Misses Azubike and Okorie chatted. When we got to my village, Miss Okorie invited everybody to meet Mom and Dad.

When school began on Monday after the Easter holidays, I went to clean Miss Azubike's kitchen then Erika walked in and said, *"Mom left today, she said that she met your parents, and wants you to visit her during the mid-year break,"* she said.

First thing in the class, Miss Azubike told the class that she had attended Amankalu Methodist Church on Sunday and met Mom and Dad. *"His father makes the best palm wine,"* she added. On Fridays, during the school-cleaning period, Miss Azubike would invite me to assist Erika to fetch water from the spring valley. Then in June, before the midyear examination, Miss Azubike wrote a letter to Mom and Dad seeking permission to take me home with her for the holidays. Mom and Dad approved, and I was overjoyed. On the last Friday before the break, I arrived at school and went straight to Miss Azubike's house to help Erika pack. When the school closed, Miss Azubike came home in a white car. Then we drove straight to her home in Isukwuato. On our arrival, her mother picked me up like a small boy. I spent the week with her family, played soccer with kids, and helped Erika and her mother with everything I possibly could. I enjoyed my time there.

Throughout the break, I did not see much of Miss Azubike. Similarly, Erika was out with her friends most of the time, but whenever she was home, she took me around the village to meet her friends and relatives. I spent most of the time with Mrs. Azubike, while she sat in the living room knitting and outside gardening.

On the last day of the break, we had fried plantain and black eye peas for breakfast. Getting ready to depart, Mrs. Azubike stooped down and whispered into my ear; *"My daughter likes you,"* so I turned around and saw Miss Azubike watching us with a smile on her face. Getting into the car, Mrs. Azubike pulled me back and hugged me. *"You are a delightful boy,"* she said. It made me feel warm and happy, and I had a smile on my face for the entire ride home.

When we returned on Sunday, it was too late for me to go home, so I slept at the teachers' quarters with Erika. Before we left for the break, Erika had washed my school uniform, so it was clean and ready to wear to school. Early Monday morning, Erika and I swept the building and prepared breakfast for Miss Azubike, then we left for school. The first thing that morning, Miss Azubike announced the result of the midyear examination and encouraged us to work harder.

I hadn't seen Mom, Dad, and Anyele for a week and is the first time I had left home, so I was anxious to get back. Finally, I got home, got a tight hug from Mom and grabbed Anyele, tickling him as he tried to run away; I enjoyed messing with him. At dinner, I told Mom and Dad all about the trip. Dad hoped I behaved myself and Mom rubbed

THE AUDACITY OF DESTINY

my head and smiled without saying a word. The school year ended with the announcement of the final exam.

    The New Year began on Monday with a lesson in writing; we started writing with pencil and paper instead of chalk and slate and felt all grown up.
    One thing that jumped at me, though, I realized I could not write, I could not get my "j" and "y" to curve correctly at the bottom of my "f" to curve correctly at the top, as such, was the child Psychologists' perfect stereotype of The Early Childhood Creativity Deficiency Syndrome. Therefore, I spent lots of time with Oyidiya at home, learning how to write. I did not have any problems in arithmetic, but to my surprise, most of my classmates found arithmetic very difficult but wrote perfectly well.
    One day in July, soon after a lunch break, classrooms began to shake, and the gray clouds became darker. The wind blew dirt around, tossing books on top of the desks out of the class. Easels fell apart, and kids screamed and ran for cover. It was chaotic; torrential rain fell, and the wind grew stronger, blowing water into the classrooms. Classroom walls were only four feet high, so we couldn't stop ourselves from getting wet.
    Notably, Mr. Okocha walked around in the rain without an umbrella from one class to another, guiding students with the aid of their teachers to the senior classrooms—the only building with walls reaching the roof. The rain stopped abruptly, and the high wind subsided. So school closed, and kids went home all drenched.
    At home, parents waited anxiously to see their children. They had experienced the same rare occurrence, and we were equally eager to get home and tell the story. *"Are you OK?"* Mom asked. *"Oh, you are soaked wet. Let me take your clothes off."* She took my clothes off and prepared pepper soup, which I ate and went right to sleep. Dad came home drenched too. Everybody had experienced the same stormy

weather.

For one thing, nothing happens in this town without a superstitiously charged rationale. So, in this case, villagers scrambled to come up with a convincing reason for the storm. Shortly, the elders concluded that God was sending a message of some sort, but they did not know what the message was or the recipient. *"Young people were deviating from the traditional culture,"* some elders proffered. In the end, they agreed to offer sacrifice and libation to God. The sacrifice would turn out to be a wonderful feast for the kids.

Setting aside, the reason for the sacrifice or how the elders executed the sacrifice, the whole event was a meat-eating feast for the kids. The elders prepared sumptuous meals everywhere in the town with goats and white fowls, and the kids ate to their fill.

Despite the joy of feasting on goat and fowl, something nagged me. I was nine, certainly too young to worry over the social inequities but there was one thing which perplexed me. I wondered why women cooked for their families every day but not the sacrificial meal. Then it became apparent to me that our culture treated women with profound disregard, even girls—my cousin being one of them.

A few days later, while Dad sat in his comfortable spot at the square, I sat by his side partly aware that his earth-shaking voice could send me flying or he'd give me a deadly warning look, which itself could be enough to hurt my feeling. Either way, I had a question on my mind he alone could answer. So I looked at him, walked away, and came back and wondered, *"How easy it would be if Mom were there to cast her shield over me."* Then I mustered enough courage and popped the question; *"Dad, how come only men celebrated the sacrifice and ate the meal they cooked without women?"*

Dad looked at me in wonder, got a little more comfortable, and told me to sit closer. Then he began to preach. I have to say; it was like a gospel according to Ikebie Ndukwe. *"There's something you must understand about our culture, son,"* he said. *"It has been this way before I was born, it will be this way after I'm gone, and probably it will remain the same by the time you're my age. You do what the*

THE AUDACITY OF DESTINY

culture demands. However, you treat your wife and daughters the way you want. Don't go out there and start trouble." Dad's answer was short, and from his tone and final advice, I believe he took the question well. That he practices the words he uttered was not lost on me either—I have watched him treat Mom with reverence, deference, and affection. I never saw any other man display.

The last day of each school year came with anguish, agony, and a crushing headache. I discovered that suspense, uncertainty, and the result of the final examination compounded by the venue and method by which teachers announced it—could force a child to suspend play and enjoyment of life and yield to the fear and agony of failure. I also learned that expectation and reality often diverge, even when the outcome seems inevitable.

Going home on that day presented its unique challenges. The overly excited and happy kids who excelled in the exam found themselves in an awkward situation. So the balancing act of encouraging the less elated kids and consoling the sobbing made going home together on that day the most dreadful of all things a child can go through.

Last year, I had not been happy about coming third in the class; then this year, I took the first place I had always wanted, but still, I couldn't express my joy. I was unable to reconcile painful and conflicting emotions. So I ran into the bush, pretended to be taking care of business until my mates went far ahead. Then I walked home slowly behind. Mom's stomach had become big again; she'd place my hand on her belly to feel the baby's movement a million times—something I hated but did to please her.

I got home from school on a beautiful day, and Mom had given birth to a baby girl, Nwakaego. Then I walked into Mom's bedroom and saw her smiling—she looked so happy and beautiful. I hugged Anyele and lay beside the baby for a while, admiring her and shaking her tiny, soft hands.

For reasons I do not know, I'd become a hand-grabber—not everybody's hand, just Uncle Emeke and Uncle Okereke's; not even a

Chuks I. Ndukwe

few other uncles I was expected to grab. Every time I saw my uncles coming to visit Dad, I'd run and grab their hands, and we'd swing it back and forth until we got to my house. Then I'd sit by Mom and listen to Dad and uncles yap as they gulped Dad's special palm wine.

    Similarly, when they decide to go home, I'd grab their hands, and we'd swing it back and forth while they asked me questions about school and my feelings about my teachers.

Chapter 3

THE AUDACITY OF DESTINY

Magic Moment

All of us have moments in our childhood where we come alive for the first time. And we go back to those moments and think, "This is when I became myself.

~ Rita Dove

Chuks I. Ndukwe

Instantaneous Reaction

If you find yourself drawn to an event against all logic, go. The universe is telling you something.

~ Gloria Steinem

Standard Four (fourth grade) was, in many ways, a remarkable class for me. Mr. Nwabeze was the teacher I had hoped to have. Sitting in his class and watching him evoked a sense of ridiculous pride in me—a feeling which spoke to me and said, *"You must be your best."* Besides his expertise as a teacher, he was handsome and tall, and everybody liked him for the friendly smile, he flashed each time he walked into the classroom.

Soon after school began, Mr. Nwabeze propped a merit board beside the blackboard. He conducted examinations on Fridays, announced the result on Mondays, and posted the first three names in the order of merit on the merit board.

That merit board encouraged us to study hard all year without pressure from Mr. Nwabeze.

The first time I saw a train, I was going home with Mr. Nwabeze to spend Easter break with his family in Ovim. I saw a big, long black object moving along in the bush like a snake but blowing smoke and horn. My eyes popped wide open and were transfixed on the moving object as it sped away. I turned to ask Mr. Nwabeze what the object speeding away from us was and turned away immediately—don't ask me why. But I could not help myself for long, so I turned around again and looked at him. Then he told me that it was a train. *"They burn coal to make steam to drive it,"* he explained. His explanation was too complicated, so I did not ask any more questions.

We arrived at Mr. Nwabeze's home early in the evening; he

THE AUDACITY OF DESTINY

introduced me to his mother and his family members. Then his sister Elizabeth, who was about twelve years old, led me to a room and told me that her name was Liz. A few minutes later, her mother sent for me. *"Take your bath and join us for dinner,"* she said. I bathed and joined them soon after.

The next day, Liz took me to sightsee around the town. Sensing my curiosity, she led me to the train station and showed me around. Suddenly, Liz grabbed my hand; *"Look over there! The train is coming, stand by me,"* she said. The giant, long train with a black engine similar to the moving object I'd seen a day before and got struck with wide-eyed wonder rolled into the station amid loud noise and stopped. Many people disembarked, and many others boarded the train.

The following day, Mr. Nwabeze showed me the Methodist bookstore—where all the Methodist schools got their textbooks. He bought pencils, a ruler, and a notebook for me. Then we attended church on Sunday and returned home in the evening. One invaluable lesson I learned listening to Mr. Nwabeze chat with his friend during the break was, *"Mistakes always occur."*

I felt as though Mr. Nwabeze took me home to teach me that lesson I'd not have learned in the class—in the manner I'd never forget.

My next teacher in fifth grade was Mrs. Helen Okocha, the headmaster's wife. She conducted impromptu tests and did not announce the results; instead, she counseled students who did not do well.

On Sunday, a week before the midyear examination, Mr. and Mrs. Okocha attended Amankalu Methodist Church. Then after church, they accompanied Uncle Okereke and Azik to my house. Dad served his Sunday delight—undiluted palm wine, while Mom cooked her Sunday special. I tended to them pretending that I wasn't me; that I wasn't the child who sits in the front row of the class and idolized the husband and wife. Although nervous, I managed occasional smiles.

Before they left, Mrs. Okocha chatted with Mom and asked for permission to let me stay with Mathew and Lydia at the teachers' quarters during the break. Mom and Dad discussed the matter with each other for a while and accepted their invitation. Then Mrs. Okocha told me I'd be spending the break with her relatives, Mathew and Lydia, at their school residence. *"Don't forget to bring some casual clothes to school on the last Friday before the break,"* she said.

During the midyear examination, one thing I dreaded more than failing the exam was disappointing Mrs. Okocha. So for every subject's test, I was the last person to leave the classroom. Some students finished their answers in half the time allocated for it. In most cases, I finished at the same time as they did, but then I'd remember the lesson I had learned from Mr. Nwabeze; *"Mistakes always occur."* So I kept on going over my papers, scanning for mistakes, until Mrs. Okocha reminded me that time was up and that I had to hand in my answer sheet. Then I'd stroll to her desk and hand my paper to her and get pampered with her pronouncement: *"Good job, Ikebie!"*

On the last Friday before that midterm break, she posted the result on the notice board; it is a pass or fail term exam by tradition, and I was relieved to see my name in the 'pass' column. Then a few hours later, Mr. and Mrs. Okocha left. For the most part, though, it was a fun week spent running around the school, playing soccer and watching Lydia jump ropes with her girlfriends. Six months later, we had the final examination, and the school closed two weeks later.

Now I was on my way to standard six—my last year in primary school. When school reopened, the headmaster, Mr. Madubike Okocha, became my teacher. I recall the first time he walked into the class and how scary he looked to me.

"I am the headmaster of the Alayi Methodist Central School," he said proudly. *"My job is to guide you, and yours is to study and learn. I encourage you to ask any question because the one you fail to ask maybe the one that causes you to fail your exam. So ask, and you'll get the answer."* Then he told us to bring out our composition notebooks and write an essay on how we had spent the Christmas holidays. *"Put your notebooks on my desk when you finish, face down,"* he instructed.

THE AUDACITY OF DESTINY

When we finished writing the essay, we placed our notebooks on his desk face down, as per his directions. *"You can pick your notebooks up after lunch break,"* he said.

Coming back from the lunch break, we picked up our notebooks in which we saw his comments that varied from "redo," to "good," to "very good." He had commented "redo" in red ink while the other comments were in black. If you had gotten "redo" as his comment, you had to rewrite the essay and hand it in before going home that day.

On Monday morning, the headmaster walked into the class looking the most imposing he'd ever appeared. He conducted his roll call and informed us we'd be having American visitors in the afternoon—scientists from America who would be spending a few months in Alayi to conduct an oil exploration. *"They will conduct a demonstration in this classroom,"* he said, *"so come back before the afternoon roll call."*

We had scarcely seen the word 'scientist' in the textbook but didn't know that we would meet one in person. Lost in a zone of intense anticipation and anxious to hear what the scientist had to say, we waited impatiently. Suddenly, a car entered the school compound and went straight to the headmaster's residence. Then a big, tall black man and a white man carrying a box got out of the car and walked into the classroom. Mr. David Marshal introduced himself and his companion Henry Anderson as American electrical engineers. He proceeded to tell us how to generate electric light. *"Observe so you can ask questions afterwards,"* he said.

With our eyes popped wide open and transfixed on Mr. Anderson, he opened the box and took out wires, screwdrivers, bulbs, a switch, and a big battery. Next, he put the battery on the table and connected wires to the sockets, switch, and the battery. Then he inserted bulbs into the sockets and invited one of us to come out. *"Don't be afraid,"* he said encouragingly.

A child's instant jumpy reaction is often the inner holy curiosity grabbing the magic moment.

Chuks I. Ndukwe

I jumped out of my seat as if I was pushed by an inner-power with a thrust I could barely withstand and ran to the front of the class. *"Thank you,"* Mr. Marshal said, smiling gently. Then he told me to turn the switch on when the classroom got dark. In a second, the class was pitch black; afraid of what might happen, I moved the switch slowly upward, and the light came on and illuminated the classroom that was utterly dark just moments ago. The sight was magical for me. I froze and stared in disbelief for a moment; then I experienced a state of jumpiness which every child experiences when he finds a toy he loves. This electric light became my favorite toy so much so that my excited, innocent mind fixated on it and would not let go.

"Ikebie, you can go back to your seat now," Mr. Marshal said. "The light comes from the electric current inside the battery. The headmaster then invited us to ask the scientist questions."

"I have three questions," I said.

"Go ahead, Ikebie," the headmaster said.

"Can every electrical engineer make light to come on as you did?"

"Yes," he answered.

The headmaster invited other questions and waited for hands to go up, but none did.

"Okay, Ikebie, ask another question," he turned toward me and said.

"Is every electrical engineer, a scientist?" I asked.

"Yes," Mr. Marshal answered.

"Ikebie, ask your last question," the headmaster said.

"What should I do to become an electrical engineer?" I enquired.

"If you study math, advanced math, physics, English language, plus any other two subjects, and if you maintain a high enough grade, you can become an electrical engineer," Mr. Marshal explained to me.

Articulated Wish

That was it for me, so I jumped up again and shouted. *"When I grow up, I want to become an electrical engineer!"* Then the headmaster ordered students to open the door and the windows.

THE AUDACITY OF DESTINY

"I'd like everybody to come up and look at the setup, one person at a time," Mr. Marshal said.

I went up again and touched every object in the setup with wide-eyed wonder. Finally, at the end of the demonstration, all of us stood up and gave the engineers a big round of applause. Shortly after their departure, the class became a deep noiseless zone of mesmerized children struck mute by awe.

"Ikebie, why are you so excited about the demonstration?" the headmaster asked.

"Sir, I want to become an electrical engineer," I answered.

"Who else wants to become an electrical engineer?" he asked.

I raised my hand again. *"Not you, Ikebie. I mean other students,"* he said. I wrote down a few things that Mr. Marshal had said, notably that I could become an electrical engineer if I'm good at math, advanced math, physics, English language, and two other subjects. I also wrote down that every electrical engineer is a scientist.

"Can I see your notebook?" Mr. Okocha requested.

So I surrendered my notebook to him and watched as he went over the notes I had taken down. Then he handed my notebook back to me. From that day on, every time the headmaster asked the class to write a composition on the profession we wanted to pursue in future, I'd write pages describing the first time I saw electric light, and how exhilarated I had felt watching Mr. Marshal conduct his demonstration in my classroom. Then I'd always end the composition stating how proud I'd feel to light up a dark room with electric light.

> **Turning on electric light was the holy magic moment—a life-altering magical moment that defined who I am today.**

My wish of becoming an electrical engineer would gradually become an obsession—to the point that just thinking about it made me happy. Although in reality, the chance was as slim as it gets—with no discernable roadmap for getting me there. Sometimes, I'd feel like my imagination was running wild and messing with my mind; at other times, I'd feel like my wish was secure in God's sacred place where he grants every innocent child's desire and aspiration.

And yet, I refused to accept the perverse divergence between child's wish like mine and its reality.

One Friday afternoon as the school was starting the weekly cleaning, Mrs. Helen Okocha sent for me and instructed me to see Lydia, her sister. I dropped my broom and ran over to the headmaster's house. Once there, I told Mathew that I was there to see Lydia. *"She is in the backyard,"* he told me.

I walked straight through the parlor to the backyard as a privileged guest. For one thing, nobody walked through the headmaster's living room; you had to go around the building to the backside. *"Ikebie, I want you to go to the stream with Mathew and fetch me drinking water; we are running low,"* Lydia said.

"Okay, let me get permission from the headmaster," I replied.

"Go ahead, but you don't have to," she said.

I ran back to the classroom where I saw the headmaster sitting in his chair, immersed in the book he was reading. I interrupted him and begged for his attention.

"Excuse me, sir, Lydia wants me to go to the stream with Mathew to fetch drinking water. Can I go?" I asked.

"Yes, Ikebie, you can go," he said, smiling and shaking his head. As I turned around to walk out of the classroom, he handed me some money—the amount of which I did not know.

"Tell Mathew to buy some snacks for both of you," he said.

"Oh, thank you, sir," I said and sprinted out of the classroom.

When I gave Mathew the money, he bought some roasted groundnut we munched on to the stream. Getting back, Lydia wanted to know if I'd like to travel to Umuahia with them. *"Why?"* I asked. *"I think it would be nice of you to came with us." "Sorry, I can't go with you,"* I told her.

Two weeks before the Easter break, Mrs. Okocha gave me an envelope addressed to Mom and Dad. So when I got home, I read the letter that was an invitation for me to travel to their home with them.

THE AUDACITY OF DESTINY

Then Mom and Dad sat in total silence for a while, staring at each other. As for me, I was conflicted with happiness and fear—happy I'd be spending one whole week with my teacher's family and scared, of what exactly I cannot recall. As I handed the envelope back to Dad, he told me to get my pen and paper out and write the reply. *"They are in school. I don't bring them home,"* I said.

"Bring them home on Monday. We want to reply to that letter soon," he said.

So I brought my pen and ink bottle home from school on Monday and wrote the reply. Dad dictated his thoughts, and then I put his words in writing. Then I gave the letter to Mrs. Okocha on Tuesday.

On the last Friday before the Easter holidays, I went to school late dressed in my Christmas clothes and was feeling very proud. I went straight to the headmaster's residence with my travel box containing my English textbook, a notebook, a pencil, two pairs of shorts, and two shirts. School closed around noon, then a few minutes later, Mr. and Mrs. Okocha came home. Mr. Okocha sat on the passenger's side of his car, and Mrs. Okocha drove the car to Umuahia.

We arrived at Mrs. Rose Okocha's and drove up to the front of a beautiful house, which looked almost the same as the European rest house beside my school's soccer field. Then an older woman of average stature came out smiling, spread her arms wide, and hugged me.

"You must be Ikebie," she said.

"Yes, ma'am. My name is Ogbuleke Ikebie."

"Come inside the house," she said, taking my hand and leading me inside the house. It was an awkward moment for me; I can recall doing twist-of-legs dance due to the pressure to pee.

"Ma'am, I want to urinate," I said.

She pointed at the urinal, and so I managed to avoid an embarrassing accident. Then she took me inside the kitchen where she was cooking. Her kitchen was beautiful and cozy with silver pans, and pots hung all over. Without feeling and behaving like a stranger or a guest, I began to help her in the kitchen.

"I wish I could keep you here with me forever," she said.

Chuks I. Ndukwe

Meanwhile, Mr. and Mrs. Okocha had retired to a private section of the house, so I did not see them until dinnertime. At dinner, I helped Lydia set the table. Then I gave everybody their napkins before I sat down. For whatever reason, I completely forgot that I was a visitor and kept helping Mama Rose as if I, too, were a family member. I felt her smug aura of sweetness that made me feel like one of hers.

"Ikebie, say the grace," the headmaster said.

Close your eyes, God is good. God is gracious. God, we thank you for getting us here safely. We thank you for the food we are about to eat. Bless it for us, and I thank you for Mama Rose. Amen.

"I can see why you keep talking about Ikebie. This boy is a sweet little thing. Can I keep him?" Mama Rose asked humorously.

"The time he spent Easter break with us back at the school, the only thing he did not do was cook, and he felt happy doing everything," Lydia said.

"His mother is a lucky woman," Mama Rose added.

"Are you saying I wasn't a sweet child when I was young?" the headmaster asked, returning the humor.

"Of course you were a sweet child, my dear," she replied.

After dinner, I cleared the table and Lydia, and I did the dishes. Then I sat with the family while they chatted about this uncle and that uncle and how they came around regularly begging for money.

The following day, Mathew took Lydia and me to the township, where hazardous smoke from burning coal hovered in the air while trains stopped and took off at rapid pace. The town was beautiful, large, and bustled with people, bicycles, and cars. Our visit ended on Sunday as everybody gathered around the vehicle to chat for the last time.

I will never forget how everything–houses, trees, and people– seemed to be running back as the car drove past them. Finally, we returned early in the afternoon and then I helped Lydia prepare lunch before I went home.

I recall talking endlessly about Mama Rose during dinner telling Mom that she and Mama Rose were alike. *"Ma, she called me a sweet little thing, and she wanted to keep me,"* I said. *"She was joking,"* Mom

THE AUDACITY OF DESTINY

said. *"Did you enjoy yourself?"* Dad asked. *"Yes, I did,"* I answered, very pleased. *"Did you behave well?"* he asked again. *"Yes, I think so,"* I replied.

We had a very unusual midyear examination in June. The question and answer sheets were different. The time and items allowed in the classroom were very different. The results came out with bizarre grading—"ready" and "not ready. *"Ready for what?* We asked each other but were afraid to ask the man who had assigned the grade.

Anyways, the headmaster placed students who scored "ready" on advanced lessons, while the others continued with the regular lessons. Shortly after this, all the students who'd scored "ready" except for me, received application forms for a secondary school entrance examination to fill out.

In August, they traveled to different places to take the entrance exams for their secondary school of choice. However, I was not among them because I had nobody to pay for my secondary school education, but I was just as happy to have scored "ready" which was the only important thing for me.

Nwakaego had been sick for a few months with fever. We did not have hospitals, so Uncle Okereke gave her pills and Mom, and Dad treated her with herbs, but she did not get better. I'd carry her on my lap and try to feed her at dinner, but she could not keep anything down, not even light soup. Nwakaego got sicker, emaciated, and weaker. But I continued to believe she'd recover. Sensing the inevitable, Mom began to wither away like a plant on contaminated soil. Then one night, Dad woke me up at midnight.

"Ogbu, Nwakaego has passed. Meet me at the backyard," he said.

My world—the world of a twelve-year-old, collapsed. I looked for Mom, but a crowd of people surrounded her. Then I met Dad at the backyard and helped him dig up the grave to bury her as tears rolled down my face. At last, we reached the right depth. And all that time I could hear Mom crying, screaming, and rolling around on the ground.

"Ogbu, I want you to give your sister her last bath, as you used to do when she was alive," Dad said. *"I believe she would want you to do*

that."

I managed to pick her enfeebled, flexible body up and carried her to the grave. I then bathed her and wrapped her in a white cloth, and then the elders lowered her down the grave.

From that day on, Mom—who had been a smiley, happy person—began to fade away with grief. She cried every day and every night.

"I want another daughter; I need a girl," she kept saying.

She traveled everywhere to see the native herb doctors to help her conceive another girl. She was in pain and inconsolable until she lost the will to smile. Her cheekbones became sharp, and her cheeks became hollower. Every time I witnessed her agony, tears would run down my face.

One evening, while she was cooking in the kitchen, I put my arms around her neck and looked into her blurry eyes. She was not there anymore. Who wrote the rule that a child couldn't be naughty to save his mother? So the Naughty me told her that I'd do everything girls do for their mother if she'd stop sleeping with Dad. *"I don't want you to die,"* I said, crying.

She hugged me and held me tight for a while, and then she looked back into my eyes as tears ran down her face and mine.

"Okay, let's cook," she said.

Then I told Egbichi that I had given up all the boyish funs and that I'll be my mom's daughter from now on. Then she retold her mother and other girls what I'd told her. Every day after school, I'd follow the girls to the stream to fetch drinking water, and I'd grind condiments for Mom to cook with when she got home from the farm. I went with the girls to the farm to fetch firewood for cooking, and I cracked palm kernels for Mom. I surely did not understand how deep Mom's maternal pain was; actually, there is something about a mother having a real daughter I did not know of, so I could not fill the void try as I did.

A few days later, Mom called me to the kitchen and told me that she'd do what I requested. A few months had passed, Mom is in a different place, and then Christ Apostolic Church held an open prayer meeting at the square. They sang and danced, and their pastor preached

THE AUDACITY OF DESTINY

to the crowd. After the meeting, their visiting missionary from America pointed at Mom and invited her to worship with them on Sunday. She went to church that Sunday and came home a different woman.

She began to attend Bible studies, prayer meetings, and church services. Surprisingly, she did not ask me to go to church with her. Was it her mother's instinct? Perhaps, she knew how awkward it would be for me because I loved attending Methodist church with Mama Ugo—my surrogate mother and Uncle Okereke's wife.

It did not take long before Mom's spirituality began to emerge and glow like light on a foggy morning. All the girls in the village, who had heard what I was doing for Mom, came to our house every evening and filled our pots with water and got all the cooking ingredients ready for Mom.

> **They would not let me give up the pleasure other boys were having. I think about it, and what comes to mind is that girls are angels.**

Some days they even cooked for my mom. Gradually, Mom regained her happy demeanor and let those girls come around when she was home so she could entertain them.

Chapter 4

THE AUDACITY OF DESTINY

The Inner-guide

If your eyes dwell in your heart; then your inner voice will be your congenial Guide.

~Kristian Goldmund Aumann

THE AUDACITY OF DESTINY

Screaming Inner Voices

Don't let the noise of others' opinions drown out your own inner voice.

~ Steve Jobs

Lest you think that I'm crazy to think we all hear voices of some sort in our heads and dismiss them as noise or a crazed old author who believes we all get signals in various forms and dismiss them for lack of the skill and ability to interpret them. I remind you of that girl on *America Got Talent*; she'd only sang in the choir on Sundays. But her inner-voice tells her to audition for the show, she heard the voice, went there, blew the roof off, and became an instant celebrity. I wonder how different her story would be today if she did not take action when her inner-voice urged her to audition for the show or heed someone's advice to do so.

The year I graduated from standard six (sixth grade) was the pivotal year in my life—the year and the moment in time when the two American engineers, Mr. Marshal and Anderson, conducted their demonstration in my classroom and took my heart with them.

The weather was chilly and gray, as fog mixed with clouds to fend off the sun. Bonfires lit up across the town to keep the villagers warm and prevent their skin from cracking. It was my graduation day, and I was about to leave home. However, a confluence of certain intervening events that transpired sent me into a dungeon of mental pain and emotional upheaval that felt like a sudden car crash.

The pain of my sister's death weighed heavily on my mind, the fragility of mom's health left me fearful and paralyzed, and departing from

Chuks I. Ndukwe

Mr. and Mrs. Okocha's family had me feeling insecure.

Somehow, I managed to make it safely home. I watched a group of girls entering my house with containers of drinking water. *"Every pot is full of water,"* Ejije said. *"We will come back with firewood."*

Overwhelmed by the girls' free expression of caring for my mom, tears rolled down my cheeks. Then Ejije wiped away my tears and asked why I was crying.

"Nothing—seeing you are helping Mom and filling the void my sister left in my mom's heart brings tears to my eyes," I said.

"We like what you're doing for her, and we love her too," she said.

Should I ever show deference to a girl or demonstrate passion you think is undue, now you know my reason. I've come to believe that girls are different from boys in many ways—in my opinion, they are God's angels.

Mom had gone to pray for a sick young girl in a nearby compound. When she got home, some girls who'd been cooking in her kitchen tried to leave immediately, but she stopped them and had dinner with them. Then a few weeks later, I went to Aba to live with my brother.

Moments of Encouragement

One week later, on a Sunday, after arriving at Aba, I visited Uncle Emeke Chima. He told me he was a member of Bende Divisional Council education committee and invited me to their meeting in Ozuitem on the date he wrote on a piece of paper. *"We are interviewing candidates for teacher training, and I hope to see you there,"* he said.

Three days later, Mr. Madubike Okocha sent me a letter telling me to come back home and see him. I was thrilled to hear from him, especially. Then two days later, on Friday morning, a Peugeot 404 station wagon drove up to the front of our house, and Uncle Anyele Aka rushed into the house.

THE AUDACITY OF DESTINY

"Where is Ogbuleke?" He asked.
"I am right here, uncle," I said.
"Are you ready?" He asked.
"Yes, uncle, I am ready."
"Okay, get in the car," he ordered.

I waved at everybody and got in the car. It was a beautiful ride home with only one stop at Umuahia Motor Park to refill the tank. At about noon, I was back home with Mom and Anyele. Then I told her what Uncle Emeke had said about going to Ozuitem for an interview and the letter Mr. Madubike Okocha had sent me.

"He came here looking for you. You must go and see him on Monday," Mom said.

When I arrived at Mr. Okocha's residence and knocked on the door, he opened the door with his eyeglasses hanging down on the tip of his nose, bent his head slightly down, and looked at me from the top of the glasses—a familiar pose.

"Come in, Ikebie. Do sit down," he said.

Mrs. Okocha came out then, and I stood up quickly to greet her.

"When did you come home?" She asked.
"I came home yesterday," I answered.

"Ikebie, I filled out an application form for you to take the entrance examination for the Government Trade Center Enugu," he said. *"There is only one of its kind in the whole region, and I believe you have the best chance of getting into that institution. They admit only the brightest students."*

If you haven't heard of good news turning to ridiculous sadness, this is one example of it. I did not know anybody in Enugu and didn't think Dad could afford to pay for my trip to Enugu either. So tears rolled down my eyes.

"Why are you crying?" He asked as Mrs. Okocha looked on.

"I know you want me to be successful. But I can't, I am sorry I can't make you proud of me as you want," I said.

"Stop crying," he said. *"If you are invited to take the exam, I will pay for your trip to and from Enugu, and I will also give you pocket*

money. And the school gives applicants places to stay." His kind gesture was as close as you can get to the window to take a glimpse into the teachers' soul. *"Are you hungry? We have food leftover from lunch,"* Mrs. Okocha added.
"No, ma'am, thank you, I'm not hungry," I replied.
"Don't leave home; I will send for you when I get the invitation," he advised.

    I cannot remember exactly how I got home. But my best guess is that I ran all the way, and judging from my past behavior under similar euphoric states of mind, I probably hopped from one side of the road to the other kicking any plant that dared stick its branches onto the roadway. About staying home—I did not. I probably would have died if I'd disobeyed Uncle Emeke. After all, there was no guarantee GTC would invite me to take the entrance exam, let alone pass the exam.

    On the day of the teacher training interview, I traveled with a group of young people to Bende Divisional Education Office in Ozuitem. A few of them had graduated from standard six (sixth grade) a few years or more before me. We walked a very long distance—about fifteen miles—traversing the farmlands.

    During the interview, I faced the harshest questions from my uncle as though he forgot I was only twelve, or maybe he wanted to eliminate any doubt as to why he'd recommend me. So, I was selected to attend the teacher training course.

    The educational system was a free, universal system, and we were the first group of teachers in the system. The teacher training—crash-course started on Monday and lasted for four weeks, ending with material preparation and a teaching demonstration. On the last day of training, the divisional education officer, Mr. C. U. Okereke, addressed the trainees and awarded us teaching diplomas. Then we went home and waited for teaching assignments.

    The following Sunday, Mr. and Mrs. Okocha attended church at Amankalu Methodist Church. Then after the service, Mr. Okocha gave me a letter—an invitation to the GTC entrance exam. Then he invited me to come to his residence on Friday before the day of the examination

THE AUDACITY OF DESTINY

with my travel box. *"Mathew will take you to the Ovim train station, where you will board the train to Enugu. I will tell you all about your trip when you come on that Friday,"* he advised.

On that Friday, I went to Mr. Okocha's residence and received instructions and money for my travel. The following day, I rode with Mathew to Ovim, boarded the train to Enugu, arriving at Enugu train station late in the evening, and took a taxi to GTC.

Then I reported to the security office for validation of my invitation letter after which a man escorted me to a dormitory where sixteen other candidates were residing. The campus was full of candidates from all cities and towns in the Eastern Region of Nigeria—each vying for the chance to take the final exams.

The written and oral examinations took place on Monday. Then on Tuesday, we took the practical tests. Each candidate had one minute to assemble five objects like the ones on a picture with pieces of wood and other materials.

Out of the five objects, I can't remember finishing any before I heard a mean-looking man say in an icy and chilling voice, *"Time is up; you can go," "Next!"* I left the room with tears in my eyes; it was apparent I had flunked it. The only question now was how badly did I flunk it? Surprisingly, when I joined the other candidates who'd gone through the nightmare, everybody was sobbing and wiping away their tears.

"I'm in good company," I thought.

"How many did you complete?" A few candidates asked.

"Not even one," I answered.

"Yeah, me too," other candidates echoed.

We stayed separated until the last candidate came out of the hall. Then the principal who seemed to lack sympathy came out, stood in front of the sobbing candidates, and informed us, *"This is the end,"* he said. *"You will be informed in a letter if you have been chosen to come back for the final examination. Have a safe journey home and Good luck in the next exam."*

Chuks I. Ndukwe

When I boarded the train on Wednesday morning, I was numb, petrified, and oblivious to what was going on inside and outside the train. I arrived at Ovim train station at twelve-thirty p.m. and disembarked the train, hopeless and subdued.

"*Ikebie, what is wrong?*" Mathew asked.

"*Everything is wrong. I wish I didn't go for that stupid exam,*" I said.

"*What happened?*" He asked.

"*I failed the exam.*"

"*You don't know that. You always look pitiful after exams,*" Mathew said.

"*Yes, but this is different,*" I replied.

We returned home at the headmaster's residence, and there he was on the verandah, reading a newspaper.

"*Good afternoon, sir,*" I greeted him.

"*Ikebie, how did it go?*" He asked.

"*Terrible, sir,*" I answered.

Then Mrs. Okocha joined us at the verandah and took her seat.

"*What made it terrible?*" She asked, kindly.

"*I don't think I did well,*" I answered.

"*Tell us about the whole process,*" she demanded.

"We did write an oral examination on Monday," I said.

"*Did you answer all the questions on the written part?*" She asked.

"*Yes, ma'am,*" I said

"*Did you have enough time to go over your answers?*" She asked.

"*Yes, ma'am.*"

"*In the oral part, how many questions did they ask you?*"

"*About ten questions,*" I said.

"*Did you answer all the questions?*"

"*I did, ma'am.*"

"*Give me one example of the questions they asked,*" she demanded.

"*The interviewer wanted to know my two most favorite subjects.*"

"*What did you say?*" She asked.

"*Mathematics and physics,*" I said.

THE AUDACITY OF DESTINY

"What other questions did he ask?"

"He asked me what I thought would happen if I kicked a ball at the wall and why."

"And?" The headmaster asked.

"I told him that the ball would bounce back with the equivalent force; I kicked it because, for every action, there is an equal, and opposite reaction."

"Go on to the technical tests," she said.

"On Tuesday we did practical tests. They gave me pieces of wood and other materials to assemble five objects in a picture. I had only one minute to replicate each of the five objects on the picture."

"Like a blueprint," Mr. Okocha said, looking at his wife.

"How many did you finish?"

"I don't think I finished any of the objects," I said.

"How about the other candidates?" She asked.

"Everybody sobbed after the tests," I said.

"Don't worry anymore," she said.

"I think you did well," Mr. Okocha added. *"Go home and get some rest."*

A few weeks later, Mr. Okocha sent for me and gave me a letter from GTC that read something like:

> **Congratulations, you have been selected to come back for the final examination on the date specified. I look forward to seeing you again.**

"Come here on the Friday before the final exam; we will repeat what we did the last time," he said. The final examination comprised of English language, mathematics, and physics with a few minutes break between them, and each subject lasted for one hour. The school had a lovely soccer field, so we spent Tuesday on campus and played soccer all evening.

Then on Wednesday, I boarded the train back home as Mathew waited for my arrival at Ovim train station. I disembarked not as grumpy as the last time.

"You look cheerful," Mathew commented.

"I don't feel bad at all," I said.

When we arrived home, Mr. and Mrs. Okocha wanted to know if I answered all the questions for each paper.

"Yes, ma'am, and I reviewed my answers three times on each occasion," I said.

"This is it," Mr. Okocha said. *"If we get another letter from the school, you are in."*

Nigeria had just gained independence, and the federal government established a free, universal education system because primary education was not tuition-free until then, hence divisional education authorities were recruiting candidates with a minimum qualification of standard six (sixth grade) to teach in the new system. I had received my assignment to teach at Okpufu Universal Primary School.

As school got underway and I'd begun to enjoy teaching the kids, Mr. Okocha sent me a letter from the Ministry of Education Enugu that read something like:

> **Congratulations. You have been selected to attend this historic institution beginning on the above date. The school is free, and you will receive pocket money weekly. Plan to arrive at the school campus no later than two days before the beginning of the school term.**

Tears of joy poured down my cheeks; I forgot I was a teacher and made a fool of myself jumping up and down. Then I collected myself and gave Mom and Dad this news.

"I want you to go to the central school and see your headmaster; let's make sure the letter is real," Dad said.

THE AUDACITY OF DESTINY

After church service on Sunday, I went to see Mr. and Mrs. Okocha. When I arrived, they were relaxed and listening to the radio as I knocked on the door.

"Come in," Mrs. Okocha said.

"Good afternoon, ma'am."

"You got the good news?" Mr. Okocha inquired.

"Yes, sir, I did. I don't know how to thank you and Mrs. Okocha," I said gratefully.

"Ikebie, sit down," he said. *"Do you remember the day you watched a demonstration in the classroom, and you jumped up excited? And every time I asked the class to write an essay on what you wanted to be when you grow up—every single time—you wrote about becoming an electrical engineer?"*

He continued, *"I am proud to be your teacher, and Mrs. Okocha is even prouder. You can thank us by being the kind of student at GTC that you're here in your primary school and go on to become an electrical engineer,"* he said, *"Lydia cooked some rice; go to the kitchen and get some. I hope to see you before you leave for GTC. Congratulations again."*

I began to cry; I could not hold it in as tears flowed down my cheeks like water. When I got home, Mom was finishing dinner, so I went in the kitchen to help her then she said, *"Go—you are a teacher now; you don't have to set up the plates anymore."*

Amidst the aroma of delicious food and eagerness to break the news, I waited until we began to eat, I couldn't help but violate one important cultural mores—to not talk while eating. Meaning, I told Mom and Dad what Mr. Okocha had told me. And immediately, Mom and I cried. From that day until the final day of the school year, I went to bed reliving the last day I spent at GTC after the final exam. I realized it would be my home shortly. Finally, I resigned from teaching.

Before I left home for GTC, I spent a week with Uncle Okereke and Mama Ugo, and two days with Mr. and Mrs. Okocha's family.

Chapter 5

THE AUDACITY OF DESTINY

Mother's Advice

When your mother asks, 'Do you want a piece of advice?' it is a mere formality. It doesn't matter if you answer yes or no. You're going to get it anyway.

~ Erma Bombeck

THE AUDACITY OF DESTINY

Teaching Moment

All you really need to do is accept this moment fully. You are then at ease in the here and now and at ease with yourself.

~ Eckhart Tolle

Can you recall one valuable advice your mother gave you—even if it seemed frightening at the time? For me, the most cautious advice my mother, Nwaka Ikebie Ndukwe, gave me was this; *"If you remain humble and keep these palms of yours clean. There is no obstacle too high nor pain so severe you cannot overcome."*

From dinner until bedtime, Mom sat near me—not by the side, but directly opposite. She had her hands around my neck and looked squarely in my eyes. She talked about God, Jesus Christ, and the essence of life and simple living—rooted firmly in humility and cleanliness of body, mind, and soul. And I'd look back in her face with an unflinching stare. It was an 'Oh! Not again!' moment for me.

No doubt, Mom was in her most comfortable domain. She has always preached the same sermon—virtues of decent living, but that time she drilled it more in-depth than ever. Finally, she took my hands.

"Ogbu, promise me that you will keep this palm of yours as clean as it is today until you return to your Creator." Then she paused. *"I know you will. Get some sleep,"* she said, pressing my head on her chest.

While my head was resting on Mom's chest, I experienced a sudden jolt and momentary loss of presence that I would never be able to explain. With that moment etched in my mind, it became a double transfusion of spirituality. And it replayed itself repeatedly.

I lay in bed awake all night thinking about the jolt and the relaxed chill-like feeling, that flowed through my body as my head rested on Mom's chest. In the morning, I ate breakfast and punched Anyele around, to watch him giggle again. I got a warm embrace from Dad.

"Be careful," he advised.

Then Mom escorted me to the motor park. Just as she was about to put my box down, a Peugeot 404 station wagon flew up the hill and stopped. Uncle Anyaele, the driver, came out and hugged Mom.

"Ogbuleke, are you returning to Aba?" He asked.

"Yes, Uncle, I am," I answered.

"Get in the front," he ordered.

I got in the car and waved at Mom, and the vehicle took off, flying. We passed many motor parks and made short stops to pick up lone passengers with light luggage.

"I've already made my money for the day," he said, "Now we can ride empty if we want." He drove straight to forty-six Ulasi Road and let me off.

"Don't worry about the fare," he said.

Then Uncle Emeke's wife, Auntie Ugo, took my box and led me to the parlor. And the time was about two pm.

"I've got to go to the store to greet my uncles first," I said. It is my usual routine. A little girl—about four years old was standing at the end of the hallway, and I had walked past her. And went to the backyard to greet my other uncles' wives and tell them I was going to the store to greet my uncles. Then that little girl screamed.

"Uncle, I am coming with you."

"Do you know where I am going?" I asked.

"To the store," she answered.

On our way to the store, she kept hopping up and down, up and down, holding my hand so tightly she almost pulled me down. Occasionally, I'd look at her, and she looked happy and cheerful. We

THE AUDACITY OF DESTINY

got to the store as customers jostled each other to get to the textiles they liked. Somehow, I managed to greet Uncle Okorie Onwuchekwa.

Before we left, he gave us money to buy some groundnut. So I purchased special groundnut roasted in oven-ash and gave it to that little girl. She gave it back to me; I smiled, knowing what that meant, took some and gave her the rest. Then we munched on our treat all the way home. Now I'm thinking. I recently lost my sister, who had filled every moment I spent with her with happiness and joy—still grieving.

And I watched that little girl break through the seal I'd wrapped around my grieving heart and occupied the vacuum my sister had left.

When we got home, she went inside Uncle Okrie's room and came out with a towel in her hands. Then she took my hand and led me to the bathroom. *"Come and take your bath,"* she said.

I took a long bath, thinking how wonderful it is for her to lift my flagging spirit the way she did. Coming out of the bathroom, I asked Auntie Ugo who she is. *"Oh, that's Tereza's daughter. Grace, come here and meet your uncle Ogbuleke,"* she said. I hugged her, and then she ran right back to the backyard. After dinner, I told Uncle Emeke that I had resigned from teaching. Immediately upon hearing what I said, he almost lost his mind, horrified, and yelled at me for abandoning the job he was proud I had. Then I gave him my admission letter to GTC and told him all about Mr. and Mrs. Okocha and my relationship with them. Then he read my admission letter and congratulated me.

On Friday, I boarded the train to Enugu and reported to the principal's office two weeks before the beginning of the school term instead of two days, as stated in the admission letter. For whatever reason, instead of sending me home, the school officials asked the security officer to let me stay in one of the dormitories. But beds had not been set up yet, so I had to sleep on the bare cement floor.

After a week, I began to cough. By the time the campus manager's office and the medical center opened, I was coughing up blood.

Chuks I. Ndukwe

So when the medical center reopened, the school nurse led me to Enugu General Hospital, where the doctor said that I had tuberculosis after hours of tests and X-rays. He then sent me to the infirmary unit of the hospital. The school nurse visited me every day, and the cooking staff brought me food three times a day. Two beautiful nurses, Iyabo and Abisola, cared for me and taught me basic algebra and English language while I was in the hospital. Uncle Okereke Chima and Uncle Okorie Onwuchekwa visited me also—five weeks after my admission.

One week after their visit, the result of my X-ray came back showing that I was well enough to go back to school. But I had to report to the outpatient ward two days a week for three months. Before I left the hospital, I arranged with the nursing staff to treat me whenever I arrived at the hospital, so I could get treatment and go back to school before the beginning of classes.

Getting back to school, the principal permitted me to leave the school campus as early as I could on Mondays and Wednesdays until the treatment was over. To avoid being seen as sneaking out of the school campus, I gave the campus manager a copy and carried a copy with me. Shortly it became clear that my lungs were infected because I could not run after the treatment. And the longest I could play soccer at full breathing strength dwindled to fifteen minutes.

On the academic side of things, I studied very hard to catch up with the rest of the class. I borrowed notebooks from my classmates and copied their notes, and I went over all the problems they had solved while I was in the hospital. My bed was the lower of the bunk bed I shared with a dormitory mate, so at night I covered my bed with blankets to avoid being seen studying because the campus light went off at nine o'clock every night, and everybody was supposed to sleep after that. Instead of sleeping, I studied under the flashlight until twelve or one o'clock every night before going to sleep.

In a strange, perverse way, my condition turned out to be a blessing in disguise. For instead of participating in sports, I focused my energy on studies and social activities. I joined the drama and the social evening clubs and was a very active participant.

THE AUDACITY OF DESTINY

I attended Anglican Episcopal Church every Sunday with my dormitory prefect, Nnyama. My impression of the Episcopal Cathedral Church on my first Sunday worshipping there was that of wide-eyed amazement at the magnificence and grandeur of the church. We studied the Bible and prepared for baptism.

One week before my baptism, the Priest advised me to select a godfather, godmother, and a baptismal name from a list of religious names. But I declined and chose an Igbo name—Chukudi—for my baptismal name, Nnyama for godfather, and mama Ugo for godmother. Chukudi means, "*I believe in God.*" It's what I say, breathe, and think with all solemnity.

On the day of my baptism, ten students from GTC sat in the front pew. It was the most uplifting spiritual experience of my life; I felt like God was right there in the church. During the baptismal ceremony, the priest called each celebrant to the pulpit, as the bishop administered the baptism. Then six months later, we received confirmation and had our first communion.

> **Although I was young, still I believed I could not have been where I was if I was not safe and secure in God's sacred place—where he keeps every child safe, and grant his wish.**

Attending GTC and witnessing Mom's transformation from a grieving mother to a woman who went to cities far beyond my village town to attend Christ Apostolic Church meetings and to pray for the sick solidified my belief.

The second half of the year was set aside for technical exercises, and at the end of the year, we had become adept in electrical wiring. So we wired different types of complicated structures following prescribed agency rules and regulations.

GTC held graduation ceremonies at the beginning of the new school term, and the permanent secretary of the Ministry of Education officiated the occasion. Anyanwu had received a scholarship to attend a university in Japan, and Nnyama a scholarship to the College of Technology in Enugu. Anyanwu was the school prefect, Nnyama, my dormitory supervisor, and both of them were residents of my dormitory. And for their reasons, they chose me as their aide.

One day, the principal called me to his office and told me I'd be attending advanced studies at GTI. *"Go over there and see the principal for class schedules,"* he said.

Therefore, I attended the General Certificate of Education preparatory classes on Mondays, Wednesdays, and Fridays. Although I did not appreciate the importance at first, still I had to comply—after all, I had no choice. The amount of work I did in the beginning at GTC to catch up with my classmates plus additional work at GTI in English, Math, Advanced Math, and Physics, was a burden I had to bear with determination.

In April, I became the secretary of the Social Evening Club. The American Consulate hosted the Collegiate Social Club, sponsored by the Nigerian-American Friendship League, so four students represented each high school in Enugu. At GTC, the president Nnyama and, the secretary of the Social Evening Club in addition to two other students appointed by the principal, represented the school. We held debates, dramatic shows, and discussions on current events televised by the Nigerian Broadcasting Corporation studio in Enugu.

In June, I participated in the General Certificate of Education (GCE) of London University ordinary level examinations and in September, I received the GCE certificate. It was strange in some ways; I had this purely academic certificate in my hand while still preparing for my technical diploma—it seemed a little weird.

GTC was an institution of highly accelerated studies—two years instead of five—so we were looking forward to graduation already. We

THE AUDACITY OF DESTINY

took our final examination in November and spent every afternoon at the regional capital or Government Secretariat, wandering from one ministry to another, chatting with relatives.

And at school, visitors from various industries and businesses came to interview the graduating students. So seniors attended interviews at the principal's conference room in groups and came back to the class without talking about the meeting. I remember seeing a Shell BP bus one day parked in front of the principal's office after siesta. Shortly after getting back to class, the principal invited all the seniors in my department to his office except me.

So I sat there alone and languished in despair. Afterwards, when the invitees came back to class, none of them said anything to me. They just sat there as if following a gagging order. Classes ended, the evening activities completed, and night sets, my heart began to race, my head burned up, and I had a pounding headache all night. I did not bathe that evening, nor did I leave the dormitory for any sports event.

Then the bell rang for dinner and amidst self-pity and headache I walked to the dining hall improperly dressed—casual dress instead of a white shirt, black shorts, and red blazer—so I had to go back to the dormitory and changed my clothes before returning to the dining hall. I managed to eat with a degraded appetite. Awake all night, I closed my eyes a million times. But I could not go to sleep until four o'clock in the morning.

I woke up feeling sick, so I granted myself a waiver from the morning physical exercises and reported to the medical center and took some pills. At breakfast, I had a few bites and went to class as usual, although grudgingly.

On my way back to class after siesta, I saw two cars parked in front of the principal's office. One car had the inscription "The Ministry of Education" on its side, and the second car "Star Lager Beer" at the back of the vehicle as well.

Few minutes after classes had begun, the principal sent for our instructor, Mr. Willington. Then minutes later, Miss Donna, the principal's secretary, came in the class, looked around, took her eyeglasses off, and looked again.

"*Ogbuleke Ikebie Ndukwe, come to the principal's office,*" she said.

I got up, shaken, and lacked self-confidence still I walked to the principal's office and paid my respect to him.

"*Please sit down,*" he said.

"*This is the student whose records you are reviewing,*" he told the visitors.

They continued to go through the file in front of them. I sat scared to death and watched the tall, dark man who seemed to be the leader of the two-person team take off his eyeglasses and adjust his tie. Then he looked at me, "*My name is Mba E. Mba. We are from the Ministry of Education,*" he said.

He continued, "*Every year the ministry offers scholarships to two students from this institution with outstanding performance to the College of Technology. This year you have been chosen for that award—congratulations.*"

"*Do you have any questions?*" The principal's question followed this announcement I had not been expecting at all.

I just sat there motionless, speechless, and dumbfounded.

"*Ogubuleke, do you have any questions?*" He asked again.

I shook my head, still in shock.

"*The principal will give you the offer letter,*" Mr. Mba said. "*You have until the end of December to accept or decline. Again, congratulations on an outstanding performance.*"

"*You can go,*" the principal said.

I left the office as my instructor walked by my side.

"*You seemed shocked in there,*" he said. "*You will not tell anybody until you have officially accepted the offer, do you understand?*"

About an hour later, Miss Donna called me back to the principal's office while still recovering from the previous shock, so I went back to the office, hoping Mr. Mba had not changed his mind. When I got there, four white men were in the office examining some files.

THE AUDACITY OF DESTINY

"This is Ogubuleke. His name is difficult to pronounce. And these gentlemen are from the Star Brewery Aba. Have a seat," the principal said.

"We understand you are from Aba?" One of the men asked.

"Yes sir, I am from Aba," I answered.

"Which part of Aba?" He asked.

"Forty-six Ulasi Road, sir," I answered.

"Have you visited Star Brewery before?"

"*No, sir, but I passed it every time I went home from the train station.*"

"Would you like to visit us?" He asked.

"Yes, sir, it will be my honor."

"We have gone through every student's record in your department, and we are quite impressed with your achievement, so we have decided to offer you a scholarship to UAC Technical College in Sapele," he said. *"After graduation, you will join our staff in Aba. How does that sound to you?"*

"Unbelievable, sir," I answered.

"You should believe it. Congratulations."

"You can go," the principal said.

> **Receiving two scholarship awards, for sure, was a magic moment of a different kind and magnitude; it was humbling, nerve-racking but at the same time, reassuring.**

When I left the principal's office, I felt like running, flying, or even screaming. After a few minutes, I felt subdued as I sobbed. I thought about Mom, Dad, Mr. and Mrs. Okocha, and my uncles. I thought how happy they would be to hear such a fantastic story. Then I realized I had not accepted the offer yet and relaxed a bit.

On Thursday, approximately thirty minutes after classes had begun. Miss Donna called me to the office to see the principal. *"I am expecting your letter accepting one of the scholarship awards presented to you earlier last week. You may decline both if you like, but I hope that is not going to be the case,"* he said. *"Here are the award brochures for you to review so you can make an informed decision. I suggest you go home and consult with your parents. Donna will provide you with a voucher for your travel to and from home. Be back here on Monday. You can leave right now."*

I boarded the train and arrived at Aba at six o'clock in the evening. The streetlights were on, and the city had never looked more gorgeous. I took a taxi to 46 Ulasi Road as the family had just had their dinner. Meanwhile, Uncle Okorie and Anyaele Ochu were lying on their mats in front of the house, chatting and laughing as they did every evening after dinner.

Getting out of the taxi, Uncle Okorie sat up and followed me to Uncle Emeke's parlor. After going through the award brochures, Uncle Emeke explained the contents to Uncle Okorie. Then both of them conferred while I ate. After dinner, they wanted to know my choice and why.

I told them, *"UAC college because I'll gain theoretical and industrial experience there whereas College of Technology provides theoretical knowledge only."*

"We arrived at the same decision," they said.

The following morning, Uncle Anyaele picked me up in his car and took me to the train station, and then I boarded the train back to GTC Enugu. On Monday, I went to the principal's office and gave my acceptance letter to Miss Donna; she typed it, and then I signed it and handed it to the principal, and he said to me, *"Congratulations. You applied yourself well in this institution. Welcome to the elite club of GTC alumni who performed above expectations."*

He shook my hand, and I left the office quietly. I was now aware that I was on my way to an institution of higher learning. Two weeks later, a day before the school closed for the year, I received a letter from the Star Breweries Aba acknowledging the receipt of my acceptance letter and invited me to visit the breweries for details of my transition to UAC Technical College.

THE AUDACITY OF DESTINY

I considered going home first to spend a few days with Mom, Dad, Mama Ugo Okereke, and playing around with Anyele. But I decided to go to Aba first and meet with the officials of the Star Breweries, Aba who had offered me the scholarship. I arrived at Aba at about six o'clock and took a taxi home. Then I arrived at Star Breweries on Monday at nine o'clock, chatted with my cousin, the accounts clerk, Sunday Oje, and met with the accounting manager.

We had a short meeting spent going over my financial arrangements: how much I would receive on a weekly and monthly basis, how much I wanted to go to my guardian, and the name and address of my guardian. At the end of the meeting, he gave me a folder containing the college brochure and the class schedule.

"Go through the brochure. You are required to be at the school a week before the beginning of classes for your orientation and room assignment," the accounting manager said. *"You will receive your monthly allowance in the second week of every month, and finally, Oje will give you a check for your first month's allowance and your traveling expenses. Contact this office if you encounter any problems."*

I left the manager's office in a taxi and headed home to the village with Uncle Anyaele, the driver. I spent a few days at home reassuring everybody I was well—that my infection did not inflict severe damage on me. Then I returned to Aba and spent my holidays at 46 Ulasi Road with my uncles and their families. Two weeks before school resumed, I went to the Star Breweries again to inform the financial manager that I was leaving for school.

The time finally arrived—it was time to head to Sapele. So after dinner, I told my uncles I would be leaving very early in the morning, and I would write to them immediately after arriving at the school; then I bade them good-bye.

Chuks I. Ndukwe

"Take some blankets so you won't go there and sleep on the cement floor again," Uncle Okorie said, reminding me of what had happened when I first arrived at GTC.

"I have a key to my room already, and it is fully furnished," I said.

"Safe journey," they all said.

At five o'clock in the morning, a large bus pulled up at 46 Ulasi Road and blew the horn. I boarded the bus and arrived at UAC Technical College at thirty minutes past two o'clock the next day after a sleep-over at Benin City.

Soon after finding my room, I realized the college did not have cooking staff. Oh boy! Was I hungry! Now I needed to cook for myself. So I asked people for directions to the market. Luckily, one student from Ghana took me across the street, where I bought some grocery. I had everything I needed in my studio—a comfortable bed, cabinet, living room set, and study—but without a stereo set.

The kitchen was huge—lined up with stoves, which students shared on a first-come-first-use basis. Then after dinner, I watched a game of table tennis at the recreation hall, and then I went home for a good dose of sleep—a perfect therapy for a man who had been on the road overnight.

On Sunday afternoon, I lounged at the recreation hall and listened to music. Then the man who had helped me get food items on my arrival came to the recreational hall. We introduced ourselves to each other (because we had not done that the first time we met) and played table tennis for a while. Then we decided to take a walk around the town.

So we walked along Warri Road and came back to the campus. In the evening, we cooked together and decided to cook together every day. That's how we began—from cooking together to doing almost everything else together. In the evening that day, just for exercise, we played soccer; we kicked the ball around the grassy green field. I ran with the ball, took Kofi on a dribble, and did not feel the shortness of breath that had prevented me from playing soccer at GTC. I took Kofi

THE AUDACITY OF DESTINY

on a dribble again around the field a couple of times. Then we went on a stroll.

We crossed Warri Road and saw a short, pretty girl with a sizeable chest and a beautiful, round lower backside sitting in front of a beautiful house across the road from the campus. It started as a friendly *'Hi'* and quickly reached passionate flirtation that culminated in unconscious seductive smiles.

"Miss, I am looking for yams," I said.

"Come with me," she said.

We followed her to the rear side of the fenced-in compound.

"Ask my father; he sells yams, his name is Ovie," she said.

"What is your name?" I asked.

"Oro Ovie," she replied.

"My name is Ndukwe, and my friend's name is Kofi. We are starting school across the road on Monday," I said.

"*I am glad to meet you too,*" she said.

"Likewise," Kofi replied.

"Okay, let me get my father."

She went inside the house and came out with her father.

"Father, this is Ndukwe, and this is Kofi. They are looking for yams," she said.

"Are you new students?" He asked.

"Yes, sir," I answered.

"You have chosen a wonderful school," he said. *"You will become managers when you graduate, seriously, every student who attended this college ends up becoming a manager after his graduation. And they always come back here in their cars to let me know I am right."*

He showed us his collection; then I chose two big yams and four plantains. We had a little faked-problem carrying the yams, so he told his daughter Oro to help us carry the items over to the school. Then I showed her around the campus which she already knew all too well. I gave her some biscuits and invited her back on Sunday to teach us how to fry the plantain.

Chuks I. Ndukwe

Oro did come back on Sunday after church service and knocked on my door. *"Come in,"* I said. *"This is my studio, and Kofi's is next door. If you want to see me any time, this is where I'll be."*

It turns out I did not have enough oil to fry the plantain. Not knowing what to do next and unfamiliar with anybody else on the campus, we decided to go back to Oro father's house and buy a gallon of oil. We were not entirely comfortable walking along with Oro—we were scared of her father, so we asked her to go home and wait for us. She went home, and thirty minutes later, we went back to her house and bought a gallon of palm oil from her mother, and then we returned to the kitchen. I had already cooked rice and stew, so Oro fried the plantain and then she ate with us. After dinner, Oro and I washed the dishes before we escorted her home. *"How is that for slickness?"* Kofi said. *"I arrived here three days before you, I haven't met anybody, and you arrived yesterday, and today you already have a girlfriend."*

"Here's your problem," I said. *"You are looking for a girlfriend, and I am not. I think she is our friend, yours and mine."*

"Are you saying that nothing will happen if she comes to visit you, and you are alone in your studio?" Kofi asked.

"First off, you and I are always together, so the chance of her visiting when I am alone is very slim," I said. *"Second, if she comes, I will call you over. Did you see how nasty her father looks?"*

"He may not be as nasty as he looks," Kofi joked out loud.

"On the other hand, he might be worse than he looks," I countered.

So we latched on to each other. Why shouldn't we, we'd found a common interest—a curvy, artistically contoured, and infectious smiley chick Kofi called my girlfriend, and I called our friend. We spent considerable time in each other's studio; we always cooked, and ate together, except when he cooked *kenke* (dough of pounded corn) which I hated.

THE AUDACITY OF DESTINY

The school began on Monday with orientation for the incoming students lasting through the morning session while the returning students started classes immediately. The school library had every material the students needed. So at the beginning of every period, we'd go inside the library and pick whatever we needed. Any reasonable person could describe our studies as riveting and intensive.

My electrical engineering instructor, Mr. Wellington, was a very experienced electrical engineer. Unlike other instructors, his lectures did not last more than one hour. He taught basic principles and derivation of electrical engineering formulas, and the rest was up to us. Kofi and I did our assignments on every subject in the classroom. I studied as I had never done before and always made sure that I covered the topics of every lesson before class began.

In June, first-year students went back to their sponsoring companies, so I returned to the Star Breweries Aba—the brewer of Star lager beer for my practical experience. I worked with the engineers and the technical staff. I followed the electrical foreman, Mr. Olatunde Olayemi, around to learn how to inspect, diagnose, and repair electrical machines and motors.

One day, I was in the yeast fermentation room with the engineers and passed out. I woke up in the hospital bed with Uncle Emeke and Uncle Okorie by my sides. Suddenly, the doctor walked in, asked a few questions, and informed me that I had zero tolerance for alcohol. He kept me in the ward for two hours, got that shit out of me, and sent me home.

So I worried about losing my scholarship due to alcohol intolerance and wondered how I could ever work at a place I'd get sick doing my job. But the 'Aha!' moment jumped right at me when I realized that some people wore masks when they worked in some areas.

On the second Saturday of January, I returned to the campus just as the graduating students were leaving the college for good. Then Oro helped me stock up our pantry before Kofi arrived. A week later, the principal gave me an application form for the Full Technological Certificate, (advanced technical certificate) examination conducted by the City and Guilds of London Institute. Three months later, I received a full technological certificate in electrical engineering.

    In June, we took our final examination before going back to our respective companies for our last practical experience. Things were a bit different this time. It was more of a "show" and "tell" than work-study. I handled all aspects of the technical work, dismantling motors and machines, repairing them, and testing their functionality. By December, I had become adept in all aspects of the brewery's electrical system. The engineers would lock in their eyes on me like a hawk as I conducted inspections and tests, and wrote reports on each work. The chief engineer came to my office a few times and asked me questions about different machines and their various phases of operation.
My work-study ended one week before Christmas, so after the festivities, I went back to school for my graduation ceremony. Then after the occasion, Kofi and I spent a week together before parting company.

    Finally, I arrived home on Saturday, January 8, 1966, and reported at Star Breweries' personnel office on Monday. Then I started working immediately. It was automatic; after graduation, my first job was a supervisor of the electrical department.

    After the chief engineer had announced my position, the electrical foreman, Mr. Olatunde went crazy. Nearly out of his mind, he complained that I was too young to be his boss. He threw papers on the floor, went to the bottling room, and stayed there until the end of the day. Then the following morning, the chief engineer invited Mr. Olatunde to his office and resolved the matter.

    My first week on the job at the Star Breweries Aba was not the happy and exciting beginning of my professional life that I had expected. Indeed, I had hoped to prove that the money Star Breweries spent to educate me was worth the investment. Instead, misdirected

THE AUDACITY OF DESTINY

anger and jealousy reigned and forced me to make a painful choice: "to stay or to leave."

Finally, I realized I could not start my professional life working in an atmosphere tainted with envy, hostility, and ignorance. So I chose to leave without even starting.

Chapter 6

THE AUDACITY OF DESTINY

Choice and Option

So, what can't you take? Decide which of the two options is harder, and do the other. That way, no matter how hard your choice turns out to be, at least you can find comfort in knowing you're avoiding something even worse.

~ Josephine Angelini

THE AUDACITY OF DESTINY

The Power of Choice

Sometimes you make choices in life and sometimes choices make you.

~ Gayle Forman

So I made my choice after deliberating for two days; Simply stated, I refused to take the crap from Mr. Olatunde with a deep sense of disappointment and guilt. I decided to leave the Star Breweries and pursue other opportunities with the Nigerian Refinery—Although regretfully.

The freedom to choose rather than be pinned down and forced to take the crap we'd not feed a rat can be empowering. It frees the soul to reach for its goal with peace of mind.

At nine-thirty in the morning, I boarded the bus, got to the refineries at Eleme, and went straight to the chief engineer's office. As his secretary tried to sit down with a cup of coffee in her hand, me being the good boy—I could not pretend not to be, dashed forward and pulled the chair out for her to sit down. Then I introduced myself and asked if I could see the chief engineer. *"I am from the Star Breweries Aba,"* I said, holding my advanced technical certificate in my hand.

She then grabbed the attention of her boss and showed me into his office. So I walked into the office with confidence, handed him my credentials, and explained the horrible situation I was experiencing. It's my "SMS" moment, and I hoped he'd be that savior.

"Sit down," he said.

Chuks I. Ndukwe

He glanced through the papers a couple of times after which he called his secretary and asked her to invite Mr. Chijioke and Ahuchogu to his office. While waiting for the two managers he had sent for, he explained the management structure and his limited hiring authority.

"It takes three managers to hire somebody of supervisory level and up—or unanimous four—as the case may be. We have three managers: Mr. Chijioke, mechanical; Mr. Ahuchogu, instruments; and Mr. Njoku, electrical," he said. *"All these three managers and I—or two of them and I—have to agree before we can hire a supervisor or engineer. I would like you to speak with these gentlemen first before I make my decision."*

My interview with Mr. Anthony Ahuchogu and Mr. Christopher Chijioke went very well. I could sense that I had their ears, but my final meeting with Mr. Njoku was one of that door-bang on a visitor's face—it did not go well at all. *"I am not looking for an electrical supervisor."* Mr. Njoku said. *"I already have Akwaja, and he is terrific. I don't know why she sent you to see me."*

"The chief engineer sent me to see you, sir," I said.

"Well, you've seen me, and my answer is, I don't need you," he repeated.

More than Mr. Njoku's rejection of me was the intense mean-spiritedness he spewed at me. So I went back to Mr. Summerlin's office, thinking, "I am screwed" and told him what Mr. Njoku said.

"It's not important," he said. *"We have already decided to hire you, but your age is troubling. However, if you can go home and have your father change your age by executing an affidavit or declaration of date of birth, we will give your application favorable consideration."*

Without wasting a single moment, I took off with the envelope he gave me, took a bus right away to Port Harcourt road, and another bus to Aba and almost crashed into Uncle Emeke who was getting home for lunch. He hand-wrote the declaration while I explained everything to him, signed it, got it stamped, dated, and signed by the city-hall clerk. Then I snatched it from him, putting my good-boy image in peril, and ran to Asa Road, took a bus back to the refinery, and handed the

THE AUDACITY OF DESTINY

affidavit to Mr. Summerlin before the day ended. After going through it, he shook my hand and said, *"Congratulations, I'll see you on Monday."*

On Tuesday, I went back to Port Harcourt to look for a flat (apartment). I first stopped at Diobu and looked for a flat-for-rent sign. As I turned onto Ikwere Road, I found a vacant room there for rent—better than nothing I thought, so I paid the first-month rent and returned to Aba.

While moving to Port Harcourt on January 15, 1966—a gorgeous bright sunny Friday morning, the bus had barely cleared Aba Township when news broke over the radio that a group of soldiers had overthrown the federal government. They named the coup organizers: Nzegwu, Obasanjo, etc. Then the news continued all day changing by the minute.

At that time, Nigeria comprised of three regions: the Northern Region, dominated by Muslims—the Hausa tribe; the Eastern Region, dominated by Christians—the Ibo tribe; and the Western Region, dominated by Christians—the Yoruba tribe. Before the coup, Abubakar Tafawa Balewa, Dr. Nnamdi Azikiwe, and Chief Obafemi Awolowo represented these three dominant tribes in the political arena.

Meanwhile, I arrived at 21 Ikwere Road, hooked up my stereo system, and glued my ears to the radio as the news flowed fast and furious. While I was in the kitchen setting up my stove, a man came in and introduced himself as one of my neighbors, and invited me to his flat on the second floor. So after dinner, I went upstairs to his flat, and there we listened to the news until late then I decided to go to bed. However, a few minutes later, he called me back to his flat. *"ND, come upstairs quickly; the news is breaking again."*

The radio named the government officials that the coup organizers had gunned down during the coup: Prime Minister, Abubakar Tafawa Balewa, the premier of the Northern Region; Ahmadu Bello, Chief Akintola, premier of the Western Region; and Chief Festus Okotieboh, the federal finance minister. *"At the moment, Aguiyi Ironsi, the top military commander, was appointed the supreme commander of the military forces and the head of state,"* the radio broadcast.

Chuks I. Ndukwe

Stunned, and unaware of the ramifications of the developing events, we lay on his couch and fell asleep overcome by the gravity of the situation. Before falling asleep, I remember Mr. Kanu saying, *"There have been numerous coups in different parts of the world; a coup never ends well. I think we are in a whole lot of trouble."*

I arrived at the refinery on Monday and went straight to the electrical workshop. There I met another supervisor—a white man, Mr. John Chamberlin. His job was to inspect the electrical systems, write repair orders and give the repair order to Mr. Njoku, the electrical engineer. *"That's funny,"* I thought—it should have been in the reverse order. He came to the workshop that morning, walked straight to me, and asked me to follow him to the substation. On our way, he tells me Mr. Summerlin does not get along with Mr. Njoku. *"He wants me to work closely with you, and very likely you'd be reporting to Mr. Ahuchogu as your actual manager,"* he said. *"Don't mind Mr. Njoku's attitude."*

When we reached the substation, which I saw was lined up with amazing electrical switch gears; I looked around, noticed that all the switchgear were Baldwin's switches, and made snappy remarks about them. Unexpectedly, my comment drew immediate challenge to prove my knowledge of the switches, so I conducted the inspection we went there to perform by myself and documented the results.

"That's fantastic; so now I can go on vacation when I want," he said.

"Why is that?" I asked.

"Every time I wanted to go on vacation, Mr. Summerlin had to get somebody from Kent in England to come over here and relieve me," he said. *"But now you can do my job. So there will be no need to fly anybody here from England."*

John peppered me with a British complement *"That's Brilliant,"* as we walked back to the office. At the moment, Mr. Ahuchogu was in Mr.

THE AUDACITY OF DESTINY

Summerlin's office discussing some relay issues at the control room when we got there. He asks about the switch, and John tells him that I inspected the machines by myself.

"OK, I want the two of you to go with Mr. Ahuchogu and check the signaling relay in the control room," he said, *"Ndukwe, see me after lunch."*

So we followed Mr. Ahuchogu to the control room to check the relay. To kick things off, I climbed up the panel, bent over the other side, disconnected the relay, and took it to the workshop to check its functionality. When I applied power to it, it worked proving that the problem was something else. So I sought the assistance of one of the electricians and got Francis Okogbuo as my assistant. We traced the fault to the control panel, replaced the push button, and resolved the problem. Meeting with Mr. Summerlin after lunch, he wanted to know if what John said about the inspection was a put-on.

"No, sir. I told John I was familiar with Baldwin switches, then he challenged me, so I inspected the switches by myself to prove it."

"I'd like you to write the test report and give it to Miss Abby," he said.

I wrote the report and had Mr. Ahuchogu review it before I gave it to Miss Abby.

On Monday morning, Mr. Summerlin invited me to his office and introduced me to a group of three electrical engineers from BP Petroleum in Kent, England, who had come to conduct a routine industrial audit. Out of all the high profile assignments I've had, that was the first. I followed them around carrying the refinery blueprint and the electrical wiring schematics. We went from one substation to another, and at every substation, I performed the actual inspections, while the visitors documented the results.

That exercise as it were, gave me the adept I needed of the electrical system at the Eleme Refinery and for fear of emergency, I kept copies of the schematics.

Chuks I. Ndukwe

On July 29, 1966, just after dinner, news broke that Gowon and other military officers had overthrown Aguiyi Ironsi's government. The coup organizers had assassinated Aguiyi Ironsi during a visit to Ibadan, the capital city of the Western Region of Nigeria. A few days later, the supreme military council appointed Colonel Gowon, the supreme leader and head of state of the military government of Nigeria. The second coup was now complete, and the federal government was firmly in the hands of the Hausas—the Muslims—and nobody could predict how the whole ordeal would end.

Nigeria was now tensed as the TV-televised incidents of Ibos killed, being killed, maimed by Muslims in the northern region, and their bodies piled up like a pyramid—it was heart-wrenching and hard to watch.

On May 30, 1967, the governor of the Eastern Region, Lieutenant Colonel Emeka Odumegwu Ojukwu declared the Eastern Region the Independent Republic of Biafra to give the Ibo people the legal right to defend themselves. Various events began to unravel. In a short time, news broke that the northern Hausa soldiers amassed at the north border were marching southwards to exterminate the Ibo tribe.

In Enugu, the new Biafran head of state, Lieutenant Colonel Emeka Odumegwu Ojukwu, appealed to Ibos to enlist in the Biafra military to raise a force large enough to stand up against the federal troops. Young Ibos, especially university and college graduates rushed to Enugu to enlist in the army in response to the head of the state's plea. I arrived at the recruiting center one morning eager to join the military, but the recruiting officer had to send me back to the refinery. *"We don't accept people who are performing essential national services,"* he said.

At the refinery, relationships had strained. John did not like Ojukwu's action; he called him an idiot, so I cursed him out and vehemently objected to his assertions, and severed relationships with him.

THE AUDACITY OF DESTINY

Lt. Col Gowon declared war on Biafra on July 6, 1967. Two weeks later, Odumegwu Ojukwu yanked every white person out of Biafra and flew into the refinery by helicopter—unannounced. Before the white engineers departed, they disconnected the electrical system, turned the plant off, and set it up to explode should Biafrans dare to mess with the plant—that is, try to restart it.

Thereupon Ojukwu's arrival, he summoned everybody to the conference room and played a recording of a discussion he had had with the president of BP of London. The president of BP had warned Ojukwu not to carry out his edict and stated:

"Biafrans do not have the skill, intelligence, knowledge, and expertise to run and operate the refinery as you'd like without us."

"Is he correct?" he asked after the recording was over.

"Nooooooooooh," we yelled.

"I want to know, can I count on your skill, knowledge, and expertise to restart this refinery and run it for Biafra?" he asked again.

"Yeaaaaaaaaaah!" we shouted.

"OK then, this refinery must be up and running within forty-eight hours from now. You must do all you can to get it back in full operation." He ordered and boarded his helicopter and glided away. Then Mr. Chijioke gathered the engineers and the supervisors together.

"Can we get the electrical system back in operation?" he asked.

I recalled that Mr. Njoku had opposed the decision to hire me and preferred his cousin Akwaja instead. So the moment of truth could not have arrived at a more auspicious moment. So I waited for Mr. Njoku and Akwaja's answer before committing myself. But time was of the essence, so Mr. Ahuchogu asked me if I was willing to take on the responsibility of restoring the electrical system.

The first thing that jumped at me following Mr. Ahuchogu's inquiry was, "Wow! My boss has confidence in me." So feeling the comfort of his flattery, I accepted the responsibility and went to work with his assistance. Saying that the major problem was the electrical power, was a ridiculous understatement of the moment. *"If we resolve that, everything else would be much easier,"* Mr. Chijioke said.

Chuks I. Ndukwe

So I went in and isolated every substation. Then I went around the complex with Mr. Ahuchogu and the electricians and turned off all the machines, pumps, and motors. Next, my assistant, Francis and I inspected every substation separately and tested it to eliminate the existence of something sinister—something that we widely suspected.

Then we began to turn the complex on, one section at a time until the entire refinery lit up as if nothing had ever happened. It's not funny, restarting the refinery then was such a tedious operation for me that if it were now, I'd perform differently. At the same time, Mr. Chijioke and the pipe-fitters had checked the mechanical structures and believed the system was set to go.

At this confidence-building moment, Mr. Essien went in with his operations people and turned on the boiler. In less than one hour, the entire refinery began to shake, releasing ready-to-explode sounds. So the operators turned the system off and allowed the pipe network to cool down. Now comes the juncture where our suspicion of something sinister came true.

After a long and agonizing traversing of the refinery complex—draining the tanks, came the discovery; Mr. Essien discovered the BP engineers had filled the feeder tanks with water and emptied the cooling tower, hence the system overheated to a boiling point. In the control room, request for our progress was coming in from the head of state's office in rapid succession.

Meanwhile, we were approaching the thirty-sixth hour, with only twelve hours to go before we'd step all over the edict and bring shame to the young nation. On a personal level, we had not gone home nor taken a break, bath, nor felt tired or hungry.

The operators got rid of the water, refilled the feeder tanks with crude oil and the cooling tower with water, and restarted the operation. Then we gathered around the control panel and watched each meter register the state of the columns it monitored. Several hours into the process, each meter captured our attention as the dials moved to the green zones, and suddenly Mr. Essien walks into the control room with a gallon of naphtha. Yes! We've succeeded in producing gasoline.

THE AUDACITY OF DESTINY

Immediately, Mr. Chijioke radios His Excellency's office and reports our achievement. High off our success, we went wild, screaming and running around in all directions. Now we were finally coming down from our high and ready to go home and bathe for the first time in forty-eight hours. Then the radio goes off.

"*His Excellency calling Refinery; come in Refinery.*"

"*Your Excellency,*" Mr. Chijioke answered, "*command successfully executed, we've struck petrol, and the complex is fully functional.*"

"Congratulations," he said. "*I had no doubt you would rise to the occasion. We are counting on you and your team. Tell everybody I'm proud of them.*"

One week after the successful restoration of refinery operation, I received a pass and military protective rank. Now I could move and travel freely without obstruction or impediment. One morning, on March 3, 1968, I went to the Okarika jetty to conduct routine inspections. The always-crowded riverside was calm and deserted. Sounds of artillery explosions sounded at a distance, and the ominous sounds of gunshots came from down the river. Shortly after this, a convoy of trucks carrying Biafran soldiers began to move toward the riverside.

I had just returned to the refinery when a plane ripped the petrol tanks apart and set them on fire. If I were stupid and dumb to think that a leader should lead even in times of peril such as we were facing, I was even more so to have joined the firefighters—without a protective outfit to put the fire out but then the second blast occurred and set my pant ablaze, and burned my legs. Shortly after that, the head of the state's office ordered us to evacuate.

The situation was chaotic, and the pain in my legs was excruciating. When I got home, all the drugstores had closed, and the city deserted. In sheer desperation, I broke two eggs, rubbed the yolk on my legs—the only thing I thought could take away the sharp disabling pain in my legs. Then I joined the crowd running for safety. For the first time I'd learn one lesson:

> **In the act of self-preservation, the body suppresses pain and fights for survival.**

So, with burnt legs, I walked over thirty miles before the Red Cross picked the evacuees up and carried us to Aba. One week later, I got a message to report at a primary school in Uzuakoli—a neighboring town to my hometown, Alayi. The villagers had cleared the location of the new mini refinery when I arrived.

On Monday morning, the management staff sent me to Egbema BP oil field with a group of pipefitters—accompanied by a platoon of the Biafran soldiers to bring back an electric generator and pipes. We took off not realizing the oil field was a war front. Nevertheless, we managed to load the generator, and a fair number of pipes on the truck before the soldiers ordered us to end the operation. So we returned to Uzuakoli with the generator and pipes and found a few columns and tanks had already sprung up.

So I sprang into action designed the electrical layout, drew the schematics, and the electricians wired the plant, and the primary school that the refinery workers occupied. A couple of weeks later, the refinery began operation.

The most momentous occasion came when the electricians asked me to turn the light on in the classroom they were staying. Can you imagine how happy and proud I felt?

I recall the moment I watched Mr. David Marshal conduct a demonstration in my classroom, and I uttered in excitement *"I want to become an electrical engineer,"* with the hope that I could one day light up a dark class. Well, that was the moment that wishes became a reality.

It was a Wow-Moment for me, as I realized this was my almost-

THE AUDACITY OF DESTINY

forgotten wish of making electric light and lighting up a dark classroom I never thought would happen—not in this fantastic fashion. So I held the switch for a few minutes, turned the light on, got on my motorcycle, and sped off without a word.

Then we operated the refinery for few months before evacuating again after the Nigerian soldiers had overrun my home town, driven a significant portion of my family members into the farmland to take refuge and carried Mom away to the faraway Red Cross camp—where she died.

After evacuating from Uzuakoli, I arrived at Amandugba Mbaise—where for the second time I'd put my technical expertise into practice. There, we built another refinery under tall trees in a thickly wooded area we thought was safe from the federal bombers.

On January 14, 1970, I was getting ready to go home for the night when news broke through the shortwave transceiver.

"Calling all sectors, come in all sectors. We have a truce; the war is over. Surrender to the federal forces; you are safe to do so."

The following day, I came to Mbieri town center, leaving behind everything, including my Honda M250 that the Biafra government had given me. Getting there, I watched the victor, chanting victory song, brandishing their guns and matching up and down. Women whose beauty are no longer seductive to the roving eyes of the men in uniform, older adults and the young in various states of opacity watched as well.

War is that rare period when girl's sensual beauty and glossy smooth skin is anything but dangerous.

So girls did not come out yet. Their war would not end until the men in uniform are nowhere around the viewing distance. Even then they'll come out disguised in ugly clothes and dirty bodies.

Finally, I arrived home that day on a Red Cross truck, and then Mama Ijeoma—who lived at the refugee camp in Obudu with Mom told me that Mom had died in the refugee camp when a Roman Catholic priest was praying for her. My younger brother, Anyele, had been killed in the battle. But Dad and my older brother, Dick survived. They lived in the bush—in the farmland hiding from the Muslim soldiers until the end of the war.

Chapter 7

THE AUDACITY OF DESTINY

Mending Broken Spirits

Sometimes a broken heart can mend something else's brokenness.

~ Munia Khan

Chuks I. Ndukwe

Cultivating Respect

Respect flows two ways and can mean as much to the giver as to the one receiving.

~ David Anthony Durham

So forget about the war–it's over, this one is for the history books, I said to myself repeatedly. But here's the kicker. There was no precedence to the events of that time. The Nigerian federal government had restarted the refinery and the fate of the Ibos who worked there before the war was uncertain. Therefore, two days later, on Friday, January 16, 1970, I boarded a train to Enugu to learn my fate and register for resettlement with the government ministries if necessary.

Disembarking the train at Enugu train station, I met Mr. Amaobi Anyanwu, my high school prefect who had received a scholarship award to study in Japan when I was a freshman. We chatted for a while. Then he led the way to his uncle's house on Ogbete Road in Ogbete, he gave me some money and told me he'd come back to see me after I'd completed the registration. As luck would have it, Anyanwu's uncle had a vacant room, so I rented it.

Talk about shock—I got a good dose when I arrived at the government secretariat and learned that I was not welcome back at the refineries. So I registered for resettlement interview with the Ministry of Education after four failed attempts. Anyanwu visited again on Saturday and took me out to dinner. Then he showed me a new building in the independent layout—a location the government had set aside to commemorate Nigerian independence from the United Kingdom. *"This building is going to be a hotel,"* Anyanwu said. *"Maybe you can supervise the electrical installation until you complete the resettlement*

THE AUDACITY OF DESTINY

process."

Without hesitation, *"YES"* popped out of my mouth, so I agreed to work for him until the government decided my fate, but I do not remember discussing how much he'd pay me. However, the amount he paid me in advance for two weeks was good enough for me having seen every bit of the Biafran money I earned during the war rendered worthless—a bitter price for losing the war. The registration process went on for two weeks. Memory loves to hold on to pleasant lived experiences and the people we know, love. And respect. So I remembered that I had made a good impression on the Ministry of Education when I was in high school,

For that reason, I sought to register with the ministry. It's a no brainer—it came naturally; my name was likely in their list of favorite citizens since they had offered me a scholarship in the past. And the work I did at the refinery during the war was still fresh in the minds of the officials. I got an appointment to come back in two weeks. So Anyanwu paid me for another two weeks.

One great advantage of doing a job the government officials recognized was how generously they could reward your performance. Two weeks later, the Ministry of Education offered me the position of vice-principal of Ahiara Trade Center. So I worked for Anyanwu until Friday then I boarded a train to Ovim, a Red Cross truck home to my village, and spent a few weeks with my family before traveling to Ahiara.

Ahiara Trade Center is smack in the middle of the village. The campus? Not quite fitting for the institution. I looked for the instructor's residences—only to find out there was none. Luckily, somebody led me to a house where I rented a vacant room located right across the southern end of the school. Indeed, it was a fitting home for a man whose time and the mission was yet uncertain.

On that Monday school started; I looked out of my window and saw students walking to school aimlessly and uninspired. The memories of all my teachers' love, their families, and the teaching crash-course I had had at twelve came bearing on the moment. I realized I would have to define my purpose and goal for being there.

Reliving my school days, the fear of not meeting my teachers' expectations, and remembering the throbbing heartbeats gave me flashes of self-doubt that I could not deny.

What is the job of a teacher? What makes a good teacher? And how do you measure teachers' success?

These are the questions I carry in my mind every morning as I leave my room in search of the answer. In an ideal world—a world in equilibrium, free of terror, where people still respect each other, a teacher is many things. From the perspective of job definition, the job of a teacher is simply this:

> **Prepare a lesson he knows well, devises the means to capture the attention of the class, and deliver the teaching effectively.**

However, this is what the teacher's job is not: sticking the material to a child's mind.

That's how a rational person would think about it. But very often, there's this other thing—the soul of the teacher. Forget about the job description. He walks into the class, and tens of innocent faces stare at him—each makes a different impression like little birds in the sky flying in every direction. Some soar, others dive only to rise again and make themselves noticed.

True, children see school as a playground. They fly like birds, and some make their way into the teacher's soul. Then for the teacher, teaching takes on a new meaning. Now I arrived at the school and looked at each student through the same prism that my teachers must have viewed me.

When classes began, the principal Mr. Peter Nwankwo, welcomed the students and the instructors back to Ahiara Trade Center. But I was struck by how coldly the staff reacted when Mr. Nwankwo announced that I was his vice that the ministry of education had specially assigned to the institution. It was obvious they thought I was either not qualified or too young for the position—that age thing again.

THE AUDACITY OF DESTINY

A week later, the school supplies arrived. Students cleaned the classrooms, the school term was all set to go, and the principal kicked off the term teaching math in the senior class. Just passing by, I noticed that something was amiss. Mr. Nwankwo's voice was drowned out by students talking to each other loudly instead of listening to him. After a while, he left the classroom in a hurry. Then came my turn to teach the next math lesson—in the same senior class made up of veterans of the Nigerian Biafra war.

I entered the classroom, hit my staff on the table, and yelled, *"All stand! Sit. Stand. Good morning class, be seated."* Entering the classroom, this was my way of seizing control and establishing an authority with which they were all too familiar.

My Introduction

After reintroducing myself, I disclosed my qualifications and the school from which I had graduated. Then I decided to give the class a jaw-dropper—a derogatory phrase they all knew was often used to describe officials who returned from Europe with engineering degrees but failed to demonstrate technical expertise— 'a been-to' so I let it rip:

I'm a 'been-here' not 'a been-to' who took on the responsibility of restarting the electrical system at Eleme Refinery after BP workers had shut down the electrical system before leaving Biafra on Odumegwu Ojukwu's order. I designed and supervised the wiring of the electrical plants for new refineries during the war. I'm here specifically to impart that technical knowledge to you here at Ahiara Trade Center.

Still, I did not think that was enough; in fact, I didn't think they gave a rat's ass about what I did during the war. It was evident that the students did far more than I did. So I went after their affinity for military rank:

I had the rank of second lieutenant, Honda M250, and a pass signed by Odumegwu Ojukwu, granting me movement everywhere without impediment.

"As with other families, I lost my mother and my brother too. I worked with soldiers, and I understand what you went through during

the war. However, you must understand that the war is over, and we cannot dwell on its spoils. Only a fool would. So come out and tell us your story," I said to them.

One student stood up and told a story about a battalion he lost in ambush. *"I was a major in command,"* he said. *"I cannot forget it, and this is my first time talking about it."* I invited everybody to come out and hug Emenike Uche. We did and expressed our appreciation for his heroic sacrifices. *"So, do you want me to teach you or not?"* I asked. There was silence, until one Samuel finally said, *"Yes, sir."* Then everybody followed.

OK, this is the rule—our rule of engagement. I'm a passionate teacher. I care a lot, and my mission is to help you like the subject that I teach—which means all that I know, love, and practice. It also means that I will do lots of demonstrations for your benefit. It will start with me laying out the topic, elaborating on it, and where the equation is involved, I will derive it from the first principles for clarity.

That's how it will be in my class—Mr. Ndukwe will be running back and forth between the blackboard and the back seat, where I'd sit and watch you repeat the steps I've outlined on the board. I mean we don't move on to the next lesson until everybody grasps the current one. I don't believe I have a single dumb student in my class. But one thing you must do is prove that you are ready and motivated to learn.

A Deal with My Students

You are free to correct me when I make a mistake. There is no penalty for doing so; instead, it will earn you recognition. I will announce topics or lessons in advance, so you can read up and prepare for the class. Finally, you can come over to my one-room residence, study with me, ask me any questions, or ask for help. You can eat whatever I have, but you must never leave my water container empty. Is that fair? *"Yes, sir!"* everybody said.

With only fifteen minutes left before the end of the period, I led the way to the soccer field with a ball tucked in my armpit.

"Come on. Let's release the tension in our bodies," I said.

THE AUDACITY OF DESTINY

We ran around the field, kicking the ball, dribbling, attacking, and passing to whoever was unmarked until the bell went off. Then I said, *"Get ready for the next class; we will get down to work."*

Teacher's Epiphany

I went home, watching the students and myself in my mind. I could visualize all of us running around the field helter-skelter, playing soccer, tripping over each other, like kids, and enjoying ourselves just for the fun of it. I wasn't just a teacher in that field; I was me taking a peek into the soul of a teacher. Then I felt like I'd always wanted to watch myself with those boys like I was on a school trip with them in a village far away. Yes, that day would not be the same if I had stood on the sidelines and only watched them play without participating in the game.

I also realized something else, something very profound. Something with which most people do not usually associate a teacher—his soul, and what inspires him.

In a teacher's soul, as long as he's with the students, he enjoys being with and shares the same interest—learning, the world's just one big soccer field for him to enjoy what is around him no matter where he is.

That day has certainly stuck in my mind. Those students had made me realize something about the soul of a teacher—the beauty of being together around people whose future lies in everything he says or does: it frees the soul of all burdens, invites destiny, and makes everything seem possible!

In some ways, though, teaching is like knocking yourself out with a cup of hot pepper soup, if it's cooked like Mom's soup. Without a doubt, there's a pleasure that comes out of the soul of a teacher when the students are engaged emotionally, eyes transfixed on him, and the brain is soaking up every bit of knowledge and information that he shares with them.

One day, the principal followed me to my math class and watched me for the whole period. *"What are you doing that I did not do?"* He asked. *"I am not sure, maybe you did not see them the same way I did,"*

Chuks I. Ndukwe

I said. *"What are you implying?"* He asked.

"OK, this is what I think you did not do," I said. *"You did not think of the students as young men who were returning from the war theater whose spirits needed mending."*

Three months later, the Ministry of Education inspectors arrived unexpectedly. They met with the principal briefly, then they came over to my class, and watched me teach for a few minutes. Shortly after leaving my classroom, they sent for me. *"Mr. Ndukwe, how do you like teaching?"* Mr. Mba asked. *"I am making the most of it,"* I said.

"Your students seem to be under control, unlike at other schools where students are unruly and out of control," he said approvingly.

"They were that way at the beginning, but I worked on it, and now they are as happy to learn as I am proud to teach them," I said.

"It's evident watching you and the students in the class," Mr. Mba said.

"The ministry has increased your salary to reflect your highest certificate, and your position is permanent. Congratulations," Mr. William Eke said.

They seemed pleased with the school and the teaching staff. After the inspection, the principal and I escorted the inspectors to their car where we chatted for a while before they left the school premises.

One Saturday afternoon, after riding around on a motorcycle with my friend, Gabriel Maduka, we ended up at his house for dinner. There I grabbed the Boston Globe—a newspaper he was receiving from his brother-in-law, a professor at MIT in Boston, Massachusetts USA. Then I began to flip through the pages. The paper featured an article about a scientific machine—a computer that would behave like a human being—read, write, and solve mathematical problems and do a whole bunch of other things.

Two companies, Honeywell and IBM, were registering students to learn the art of programming the machines. At the end of the article, I

THE AUDACITY OF DESTINY

read an advertisement by Honeywell Institute of Computer Science in Burlington, Massachusetts, and invites applications for its newly founded institution. Gab applied to Northeastern University for mechanical engineering. But Boston Globe's dangling-bone-at-the-dog moment grabbed me, so I chose computer science. A few weeks later, Gab and I received our acceptance letters.

Now you could see two best friends approach the same decision point from different mindsets. When we applied for F1 visa, Gab applied directly to the American Embassy in Lagos following in his brother-in-law's footsteps. My decision was a priori having had no previous experience in such matter. I submitted my application through the Ministry of Education in Enugu. Unfortunately, the embassy rejected Gab's request. But I interviewed first with the Ministry of Education officials who had no clue about what computer was, so I recited what I had read in the Boston Globe.

"We will prepare a file and inform you when it is ready to take to the American Embassy in Lagos for your visa," they said to me.

It would appear at that time when I applied for admission to a college in the US that destiny had sent its signal and I had acknowledged the message, and now, what was left? My choice to continue teaching or leave Nigeria to pursue higher education in the United States of America—again, it was a no brainer. I decided to pursue higher education in the USA.

Even the puritan utters foul language when frustrated. So I waited for my F1 visa interview appointment until I became frustrated and curse-words poured out of me like steam out of the boiling kettle. A few weeks later, the ministry invited me to Enugu for my interview and told me to be prepared to travel to Lagos from there. So when I arrived in Enugu, the (Ministry) department of education had prepared a file for me, made my flight reservation for December 9, 1972, and included the confirmation paper in my file. *"Should the consul ask for your flight*

Chuks I. Ndukwe

date, it is the date on the flight confirmation," the clerk said. Finally, I gave the clerk the affidavit of sponsorship and financial statement the ministry had requested from Uncle Okorie Onwuchekwa to add to the list of the document in my file, and then I left for Lagos.

> **The wheel of government may turn slower than we appreciate, but in the end, you can be sure to get the best advice dealing with other governments and regulated institutions.**

I decided to wire my tuition fees for one semester before the interview, which was the ministry's advice that I took to heart. Sure, I'd saved enough money with Barclays Bank in Umuahia—to pay the tuition fees hence I went there and had them cut me a bank check. So I arrived in Lagos on Friday, went to the bank with Uncle Anyaele Ochu on Monday, and wired the money to Honeywell Institute of Computer Sciences in Burlington, Massachusetts.

The American Embassy was already overcrowded when I arrived on Tuesday with no vacant seat available. So then, I waited between sitting outside and running inside the waiting room to check the call-number until the consul called my name. Now gripped by fear of rejection, my knees began to shake, almost buckled under me as I walked to the consul's counter, and handed my file over to him.

The consul glanced through every paper in my file and shot questions at me in rapid succession. Then he told me that my school had started two weeks earlier and to leave without any further delays. Finally, he sent me to a doctor for my medical and vaccination.

"I would have left if the Ministry of Education had sent my invitation for an interview in time, but I'll study hard to catch up if you grant me a visa," I said to him earnestly.

"Congratulations, and good luck," he said. *"Before you leave, you must mail a money order for one hundred-fifty Naira to the Ministry of Education in Enugu and bring a copy to this office. It should have been the first thing they did."*

So I went back to the store. And told Uncle Anyaele I had no more money left to buy the money order. Then he took me to the bank, purchased the money order, and made a copy of it in the bank. Then I mailed the stub to Enugu and kept the copy. Finally, I went back to the embassy, slipped the copy of the money order, and envelop from the doctor under his window. Then he nodded and waved.

Getting back to the store, the full weight of disbelief asserted itself as I caught the 'shaky-disbelief syndrome' I could not assist my relatives in the store. So I dropped a few rolls of textiles when they asked me to hold one end. They thought I was hungry, but it was not hunger. It was a feeling that I knew I would overcome only by the help of a good night's sleep.

On Monday, I returned to Aba for my final travel preparation. Then two weeks later, I got married, attended my sendoff parties, and returned to Lagos with my newlywed amidst toasty weather conditions we hardly embraced nor enjoyed.

Finally, on December 9, 1972, I departed Nigeria.

Chapter 8

THE AUDACITY OF DESTINY

The Journey

The only journey is the one within.

~ Rainer Maria Rilk

THE AUDACITY OF DESTINY

Beyond The Shores

The greatest thing in this world is not so much where we stand as in what direction we are moving.

~ Johann W. von Goethe

My first time seeing the airport and airplane on the ground was on December 9, 1972, when I arrived with Uncle Anyele Ochu and my wife in a taxi. People walked around listlessly, listening to the sound system for their boarding announcements. Suddenly I heard my boarding call. I hugged Uncle Anyaele and my wife, and then I boarded the plane at around eight o'clock. As I was in my seat, a tall black man carrying a garment bag walked over to my position, put his luggage in the overhead bin, and sat down next to me. Through the window, the tarmac looked serene as fog obscured the electric light that beamed over the airport from the poles—it was a luxurious sight that pleased my senses. Then after a short wait, the plane taxied majestically along the tarmac for takeoff. *"Ladies and gentlemen, the plane is ready for takeoff. Fasten your seat belts,"* the pilot announced.

The plane took off with a loud noise; its front end tilted upward and climbed into the sky. The entire city of Lagos, from the sky-view and by electric lights, looked beautiful and diminished in size until it vanished out of view. Suddenly, another announcement came over the sound system: *"Ladies and gentlemen, we are cruising at thirty-four-thousand feet altitude. The Fasten Seat Belt sign is off. You are free to walk around."*

The gentleman sitting next to me looked so familiar—it was as though I'd met or seen him before. I couldn't have, though, he was Efik, and I'm Ibo. It was his look—he looked like my brother, Dick. Soon the cabin got very cold. He asked for two blankets, which he got. Then he gave me one and covered himself with the other. We chatted about the Nigerian Biafra war and my destination—Honeywell Institute of Computer Sciences, Burlington, Massachusetts.

"Does the school know that you are coming today?" He asked. *"I am not sure, but they sent me this letter,"* I said and handed my admission letter to him. *"All right, I am glad we met,"* he said. *"You'll stay with me till you start school,"* he decided. Following this reassuring conversation, he showed me the in-flight toilet and safety gadgets. He seemed to be pretty well-acquainted with everything which gave me the comfort and the idea that he was well-travelled.

"Ladies and gentlemen, fasten your seat belts," the pilot announced a second time. The plane moved as if it was going over bumps on the road and then, it went straight down. Descending this way was my very first experience of the sensation of free-fall. For a second, I felt my body falling into an abyss. I felt as though I was no longer in contact with the floor of the plane on which my legs rested or the seat on which I sat. After a few more minutes, the aircraft steadied again. Then hours later, I saw the sun coming out. This time, the plane descended with steady, less-jerky-over-bumps movements, and steadied again. It kept repeating that worrisome movement until another announcement sounded: *"Prepare for landing."*

The hostesses walked around, making sure all the passengers had their seat belts on, and the seats were in their upright positions. Then the plane dived and landed with a little jolt and taxied majestically to the gate.

"Ladies and gentlemen, welcome to Schiphol Airport, Amsterdam," the pilot declared. And then the pilot directed the passengers to their connecting flights. Dr. Ekong and I made our way to the terminal where we boarded the plane to JFK International Airport in New York. On arrival at JFK International Airport, the Immigration and Naturalization Services office processed my F1 visa before we took a much smaller plane to Logan Airport in Boston where, unbeknownst to me, the most

THE AUDACITY OF DESTINY

significant shock of my life awaited me. Then came the shocker. Outside the terminal—it was snowing.

For one thing, snow was something I had only heard about in the church and never thought I would experience myself. But that morning, it poured over me—in a tropical suit and the airport like rain. I realized immediately that this was certainly not the place to be wearing a tropical suit. Fortunately, Mrs. Ekong let me in the car before I froze myself to death just standing there in the falling snow—after Dr. Ekong had introduced us. Then she started the car and warmed us up. *"Take us to the mall,"* Dr. Ekong said.

Arriving at the mall, we made our way inside and traversed the entire mall before getting to the Burlington Coat Factory where Mrs. Ekong bought me a coat, a hat, a pair of gloves, and two sweaters to go with it. *"These will last you through the winter,"* Mrs. Ekong said.

I don't remember anything of the ride from the Airport to Newton, Massachusetts, where Dr. and Mrs. Ekong lived; I slept all the way there. Getting there, it was so cold in that colonial house that I found my sweater was less than adequate for the weather. So I curled up in the bed and covered myself with sheets and blankets. Not even a tractor beam could pry me out of the layers for dinner. The maid tried again to get me out for breakfast; still, I was too cold to oblige her. But after Dr. and Mrs. Ekong had gone to church, I felt wet and smelled pee—an unfortunate result of living under the sheets. Ashamed and humiliated, I told the maid when she came around again. *"It's okay. I will give you another set,"* she said, collecting the wet beddings.

"Can you wash my clothes too?" I begged her.

She collected my clothes and left the room. Then she came back, wiped the mattress off with cleaning fluid, and made the bed later. On Monday, Dr. Ekong drove to Honeywell Institute of Computer Science in Burlington and spoke to the dean of admissions and then he told me that Mrs. Ekong would pick me up on her way home from work. Classes ended at three-thirty, and then Mrs. Ekong picked me up a few minutes later. Dr. Ekong Dropped me off at school in the morning, and then Mrs. Ekong picked me up in the afternoon. And that was the dynamics in play during my first week in the US while attending school from Dr. Ekong's house for one week.

On December 15, 1972, the dean's secretary escorted me to Mrs. Terry Zdanauk's house at 11 College Road in Burlington where the school had arranged for me to live. When I arrived at her home at four o'clock in the afternoon, she called her children Dan, Andy, Renee, and Billy and introduced us to each other. *"Where did you get that funny name?"* Dan asked. *"Where are you from?"* Andy asked. *"I am from Nigeria,"* I replied.

"He'll be attending Honeywell School down in the mall area," Terry said. *"And he will be living here with us, so be nice to him."*

"How do you pronounce your name?" Renee asked. But as I tried to help them pronounce my name, they gave up before I did. Nevertheless, this brief question-and-answer moment made the beginning of my life in America memorable and gave me the comfort to live with Terry's family until I transferred to Northeastern University and moved to Boston.

My first familiarity with American people had come when I was in high school attending social events at the American Consulate in Enugu, Eastern Region of Nigeria. And my love for America grew from my love of the people who worked at the consulate and the Peace Corps who taught at various high schools.

I'll never forget one occasion when I was getting ready to propose a debate—my first time speaking in the public televised by the NBC TV studio in Enugu. As the camera was about to roll, I caught instantaneous Parkinson's disease; my fingers pounded the podium violently, causing quite a rattle. Then an American lady—the principal organizer of the event stood behind the TV monitor inside the studio, smiling, clapping soundlessly, and encouraging me to carry on until I began to laugh too. Slowly, she cured Parkinson's disease that had attacked me, and the rattling stopped. I ended up delivering a well-received proposition on the unity of Africa as the president of Ghana, Kwame Nkrumah.

After the debate, I learned that she was from the city of Boston. The next logical result of her compassion was the encouragement I felt. So I fell in love with America and Boston—the city of her birth. That's how and when my love for America began.

> **I cannot talk about falling in love in high school with America without Boston at the backdrop, or tell about my ride with destiny without paying tribute to Boston Globe for it was the Globe's media-laser-beam that guided me to where I am today.**

So I moved to Boston convinced that I had finally arrived at the place I had dreamed of visiting. I started to work for a cleaning company, joined a workers union, and got health insurance. My left eye had suffered severe damage when a sharp object hit it. It turned out that I needed eye surgery. When I visited Dr. and Mrs. Ekong over the weekend, I showed them my insurance card.

"I want to use it for eye surgery," I said.

"Okay, let's do it before school resumes," he said. *"How many more weeks are left before school starts again?"*

"Three weeks," I answered.

So Dr. Ekong made all the necessary arrangements. Then he picked me up on Friday, the day of the operation, drove to the hospital, did all the paperwork, and took part in the preliminary evaluation.

"The muscle behind the retina is damaged," the operating doctor said. *"It has to be straightened out to see how much more we can do."*

Before the procedure, Dr. Ekong wheeled me to the operation room and asked for local anesthesia. The nurse stuck a needle in me and pumped the fluid. So I was awake during the operation, feeling the cuts and stitches like gentle scratches but not strong enough to make me jump up or scream. After the surgery, I lay in the recovery room and waited for the nurse. Instead, Dr. Ekong walked in with a black pad in his hand and told me that the procedure had gone well. Before taking me home, he put the eye patch on me and told me to keep it on until I came back for a checkup.

The following day, Mrs. Ekong brought me cold cuts, vegetables, and sandwiches. Then on the appointed Saturday, I had my marathon checkup, so I did not miss any classes. *"You can stop wearing the eye patch,"* the doctor said. *"Your eye is okay now."*

I visited Dr. and Mrs. Ekong the following day after church and thanked them for their kindness. In the meantime, my best friend, Gabriel Maduka, had arrived in the United States. He was living with his brother-in-law at MIT in Cambridge, Massachusetts and had registered for mechanical engineering at Northeastern University too. So we decided to share a two-bedroom apartment located just two blocks away from the university.

My first job in Boston was at McDonald's restaurant, where I cleaned the restaurant after the evening shift. One summer night, mopping the office and dancing to the music on the radio, it hit me: John the store manager had left the safe full of dollar bills open and gone out to the club. I remember calling the regional manager Woody to come to the store. Then he demanded that I tell him the reason, but it wasn't something I could share on the phone.

"I am in bed with my wife, for crying out loud!" He said. *"Don't call me back. Okay?"* He said as he slammed the phone down. So I secured all the doors; and I sat in his office all night as though I was a security guard.

Finally, Woody showed up in the morning, counted the money in the safe, and told me that there weren't many people like me around. That was it—that was my compliment; obviously, Woody thought his comment was a fitting reward for not emptying the safe and taking off with the money.

Chapter 9

THE AUDACITY OF DESTINY

I Became Me Here

I live in that solitude which is painful in youth, but delicious in the years of maturity.

~ Albert Einstein

Chuks I. Ndukwe

Learning and Practice

For the things we have to learn before we can do them, we learn by doing them.

~ Aristotle

Northeastern University runs a unique cooperative system of education—the co-op; students spend twelve months of their freshman and senior years in school—no summer holidays, wasting time, not in the schedule, and no messing around. The university splits three years in-between between the classroom and cooperative program [work-study]. When I finished my freshman year and the first quarter of my sophomore year, I was ready and eager for my co-op program. But how a student could get the co-op job was a question that would chew at me for nights and days.

Regardless, I was comforted that the educational system at Northeastern University was no different from that of UAC Technical College that I'd attended in Nigeria which followed a perfect balance between theory and practice and the application thereof. Still, there was a small difference; in Nigeria, I was on a scholarship and knew I'd be doing my work-study with my sponsoring company. But at Northeastern University, students do not know which company they'd work for in advance unless they had been hired once and invited back.

> **For most students who walked the grand hallways of Northeastern University, serendipity often leads to the most enriching experiences beyond the confines of the campus.**

THE AUDACITY OF DESTINY

On that chilly Christmas Eve, my roommate, Gabriel, had gone to Cambridge to spend Christmas with his sister and brother-in-law at MIT. Suddenly I received a phone call from Mrs. Ekong.
"We are expecting you here," she said.
"I wasn't sure I'd be received cordially uninvited," I said in response.
"Don't be silly," she scolded. *"You don't need the invitation to visit your family. We have light entertainment by the fireplace; get your ass over here."*

So, I drove to Newton and joined the all-night party. I woke up early on Christmas Day. And the maid and I did the house chores. Indeed, I was in Christmas mood and eager to go to church with Dr. and Mrs. Ekong. But something went wrong: after taking a shower, I put my clothes on and went to the bathroom to comb my hair, then I raised my hand, and was struck with malicious body odor—loathsome enough to send my Christmas spirit into a tailspin.

I thought it was something blackish, and It was the first time I had smelled myself, and my first instinct was of shame which took over. I wasn't going to tell anybody I felt this way—HELL NO! So I ran into my room and hid there until Dr. Ekong came to fetch me. *"We are waiting for you,"* he said. *"I can't go with you,"* I replied. *"What happened to you?"* He asked.

"I smelled myself," I said apologetically.

"Did you put deodorant on after your shower?" He asked. *"No, I forgot to."*

"That's why deodorant is the most popular item in the market today," he said. *"Everybody smells if they don't put it on. Put it on and let's go."*

So I sprayed deodorant on my armpits—a generous amount of it, for that matter—and went to church. I sniffed at my armpits all day to check if the malicious odor had come back; I had never been so embarrassed and insecure.

Returning from the church, I went straight to the bathroom and sprayed an excessive quantity of deodorant on my armpits once more, afraid the malicious odor could come back. Nevertheless, we had a pretty joyful Christmas; together, we watched Christmas specials on TV and drank lots of eggnogs.

The school began on Monday, and Arthur D. Little, a software company in Cambridge, invited me for a co-op interview. At that time, I had taken courses in programming languages such as FORTRAN, Pascal, and Assembly, etc. I arrived for the meeting, filled out some forms, and sat back waiting for the interviewer. Then the chief engineer, Mr. Gordon, walked in, went to his office, and came back to the lobby.

"Are you…from Northeastern?" he asked, unable to pronounce my name.

"Yes, sir, my name is Ogbuleke Ikebie Ndukwe," I said.

"Follow me, please," he said.

I followed him to his office.

"Have a seat," he said. *"Have you taken FORTRAN?"*

"Yes, I have, sir."

"OK, how would you code this simple problem in FORTRAN?"

Then he gave me the question paper, a pen, and a blank sheet. After I had coded the program, he went to the computer room and compiled the code. Then he came back to his office and peered at me from over the top of his eyeglasses.

"Well, for a good start, it compiled. Let's see what the output looks like," Mr. Gordon said and went back to the computer room. *"It looks like you did the job,"* he said, returning to his office. *"The code worked."*

After that, he gave me a brief overview of what the company does. Then he told me to hold on. *"I'll be right back,"* he said and went to his secretary's office then I followed to go to the men's room and as I went out into the hallway, I heard him say to the secretary, *"I'd like to hire this guy, but I can't pronounce his name."*

At that moment, I made a "U" turn immediately, went back to his office, called the International Students Office at Northeastern University, and requested name change instantly. *"My co-op job is in jeopardy unless I change my funny name,"* I told the Dean of

THE AUDACITY OF DESTINY

International Students.

"*What would you like your alias to be?*" he asked.

"*I would like it to be my baptismal name, Chuks, sir.* "C" "h" "u" "k" "s,"" I said and spelt it slowly.

"*Consider it done,*" he said.

Ben came back to his office to learn. I had changed my first name while he was in his secretary's office.

"*What did you change it to?*" he asked.

"*I changed it to Chuks so you won't have any problem pronouncing it.*"

"*So how do you pronounce it?*"

"*You can pronounce it as Chucks or Chooks.*"

"*That is amazing. How did you come up with that name so fast?*"

"*It's my baptismal name.*"

"*Splendid, you can think fast on your feet,*" he said.
"*Congratulations, I'll see you on Monday.*"

I worked at Arthur D. Little for three months modifying codes, assisting Ben around the computer room, and filing printouts. On a few occasions, Ben and I had lunch at his favorite Irish restaurant and chatted about some of the professors at Northeastern University.

> **For me, education is not what we read but what we learn and remember. And knowledge is the precious principles we understand, retain, and can put into practice.**

In some ways, hearing Ben talk about Northeastern with pride and gratification gave me a sense of optimism and hope in the program. I went home one day feeling like I was hanging around with a mentor—a dignified elder who'd seen it all and wanted to pass the baton to the younger generation rather than a manager who wants to see the job done. The day my co-op ended, we had a meeting in which we spent time in Ben's office, talking about my stint with him and other things to remember, such as:

Chuks I. Ndukwe

> **Every manager loves an employee who is dependable, helpful, and diligent, and you have all those qualities. I will ask the university to send you back during your next coop period.**

Three months passed by quickly, and I was back on co-op at Arthur D. Little. Ben had taken on program simulation to determine the logical results of the code we had been compiling while I continued my previous assignment. Mostly, though, I just watched Ben and wondered about the contrast between the work I did as an electrical supervisor back in Nigeria and the work of a software engineer. I reveled in the office culture but was very conscious that I had a long way to go before I would be competent enough to do what Ben was doing.

"Do you plan on going back to Africa after your graduation?" Ben asked me once. I answered, *"Yes, I do, sir."*

"Can you find a job as a software engineer when you go back?"

"There might be such opportunities by that time," I replied.

"If you can't find a job there, you can come back and work for me," he said.

> **Ben's statement exposes, in no small extent, his limited understanding of the US immigration laws. You cannot come and go at will unless you are a citizen or permanent resident.**

On Wednesday afternoon, the office had a meeting to discuss the expiration of their contract in Cambridge. *"I see no need to bemoan this event,"* Ben said. *"We've won another contract with another company in Mansfield, Massachusetts."* According to Ben, Mansfield was about a one-hour drive from Cambridge. For one thing, I had hoped to do all of my co-ops at Arthur D. Little, but that hope fizzled out after the meeting. Then two weeks later, my co-op ended with a celebration at Ben's favorite Irish restaurant.

"Today is your last day with us," he said. *"I will transmit my appraisal to the university as usual. But I cannot be certain about our existence here in the future, because our contract is expiring. However,*

THE AUDACITY OF DESTINY

I have enjoyed working with you and learning a little bit about Nigeria. It's only three o'clock; you can leave anytime you choose."

Now confronted with mixed emotions—excellent job performance on the one hand and disappointed that I'd not return to Arthur D. Little on the other, I left the office at around three o'clock, drove along the Charles River just to watch the seagulls' acrobatic show—float, twist, and dive in the water, and then I went home from there.

Now Gab came home with the same disappointing feeling—not going back to his co-op employer. Yes, we were both in a deep funk that evening. So we went back to school on Monday, feeling less confident about the possibility of finding another co-op job. I registered for my courses, which were mostly computer programming courses still eager to go back to work and sharpen my skills in software programming.

The quarter rolled by slowly to the end as students had begun to attend co-op interviews. One day, I got an invitation to interview at TeleAudit in Bedford, Massachusetts. So I attended the interview, got the job, and came home excited to be going back to another co-op. Then Gab came home later in the evening happy with a big smile—he got a job, too! Then one week later, the quarter ended.

I arrived at TeleAudit on my first day almost at the same time that the secretary, Miss Maryann, arrived. We had breakfast in the cafeteria—tea and toast—before other workers came. It turned out that tea and toast for breakfast would become our daily ritual throughout the time I did my co-op there.

Mr. Jack Brown, the manager, arrived and introduced me to his engineers: John, Glen, and Pat. Then one hour later, two gentlemen, Mr. Jimmy Olsen and Tim McNeil, both of who were the consulting engineers arrived, and Jack introduced us.

The differences in office culture between Arthur D. Little and TeleAudit could not be starker. Sure, there was a dichotomy between the two. One involved staring at the computer screen, hitting the keyboard, and running between the computer and the printer—and the other, staring at the computer screen, hitting the keyboard, and standing by a bench assembling chips on a printed circuit board. Yes, I fitted nicely in both.

"John, let Shoots play with the test fixture until I decide what he will be doing for his co-op," Mr. Jack said, butchering my name.

I got the test fixture from John and played with it for a while—until lunchtime, to be exact. Then after lunch, I asked for the schematics, test procedure, and studied them until closing. The following day, I began to play with my toy—the first in my toy-box. First, I connected the fixture to a printed circuit board, and then I began to turn the switches off and on one at a time and recorded the light pattern in my notebook in binary format, which I later decoded into hexadecimal values.

After lunch, Mr. Jack came by to check on my progress. Then he invited his chief engineer, John to witness what I was doing. Talk of a surprise! Mr. Jack's action felt like a mother watching her son take his precocious first step sooner than she had expected.

"I was getting ready to give him a tutorial on the fixture," John said. *"Looks like you've found yourself a technician to assist Pat,"* Mr. Jack told him. *"Well, Chuks, congratulations. You've found yourself a permanent position for your co-op."*

From that moment on, I worked with the engineers checking, testing, and assembling printed circuit boards. Then one day, Mr. Jack invited me to his office just before lunch. He joked about how it feels like I'd been a permanent employee forever and asked me back for my next co-op. The day ended, and MaryAnn gave me a coffee mug as a souvenir.

"We've had quite a few students from Northeastern, and the engineers never liked any of them," she said *"but this time they can't stop talking about how you came in and grabbed the bull by the horns. I will miss having early morning tea and toast with you. Good luck in school."*

Dr. Ekong had received a job offer from a hospital in Rolling Hills,

THE AUDACITY OF DESTINY

California, and Saturday was his family's departure date, so I drove to Newton, Massachusetts, to bid them good-bye and ended up spending the weekend with them.

The quarter ended, and I was back at TeleAudit. MaryAnn arrived as I was entering the office, so she followed me to the lab, and the engineers gathered around.

"We missed you, Chuks," MaryAnn said. *"We had another student after you, but he was a sorry ass. I know Jack will be happy to see you back."* Then John joined in, *"Let's welcome the real engineering student back to the lab." "Yeah, welcome back, man,"* Pat said.

The engineers cheered, and we embraced each other like soccer players who'd just scored a winning goal in a world championship cup match. At this moment, Mr. Jack came out of his office and joined the guys in the lab. I waited impatiently, hoping John would give me an assignment, but he did not. Therefore, I went over to his corner and asked him for one. *"Hey man, you still got the VIP seat, same as before,"* he said.

I took my seat beside Pat as usual and began to tidy and freshen up the test bench.

"The system is selling like hot cake," Pat said. *"Right now, we have enough orders to last through your co-op period."*

In the meantime, Gab had finished his final examinations, taken his yearbook photos, and informed his family about his imminent return home. Then one evening, I was in the kitchen cooking when suddenly the door swung open.

"The results are out, and I am graduating!" Gab screamed.

"Congratulations," I said.

"Let's go to the bar. I want to get drunk," he said. *"You can have your favorite drink, Pepsi and drive us back safely."*

After dinner, we walked a few blocks to a bar on Massachusetts Avenue; there, he had a few drinks, and I had Pepsi. Then we hung around the bar until Gab began to lose his coordination, and then we came home and went to bed. A few weeks later Gab graduated, then a week later, I escorted him to the Logan International Airport, where he boarded the plane back to Nigeria.

Now I was at the verge of depression over the loss of my best friend and the thought of how to keep the two-bedroom apartment — so conflicted by the idea of moving out and my love of it. I posted roommate wanted signs in Laundromats and on-campus notice boards after which a few people came by to inspect the apartment with their loud-comedian-friends. Not only did they scare the hell out of me, but they also inflicted anxiety syndrome on me. So I quit interviewing applicants and gave up entirely after a few weeks of trying.

> **I also realized that living with a total stranger would undermine my simple way of living—a few visitors, water and Pepsi Cola for favorite core drink, and reasonable noise.**

As my co-op ended, it became apparent that I was now one of the guys; my expertise in testing the printed circuit boards had earned me friendly jokes and bragging rights in the lab.

Back in school, the quarter began on a Monday. Now I was in my junior year—one more year before my graduation. True, days do fly when you're having fun stuffing your brain with transistor technologies and field theory.

Like a drunken sailor, I had had more than I could handle. But unlike the sailor's slugged mind, my studies made my mind sharper, and the importance of my courses would become evident shortly.

I went back on co-op at TeleAudit and arrived just as Maryann was opening the office door; we exchanged pleasantries and had breakfast as always. The following Monday morning, a truck rolled into the parking lot while Maryann and I were entering the office. The driver approached us and asked MaryAnn for directions to the TeleAudit shipping dock, then MaryAnn directed him to the receiving platform where he dropped off a large carton on the loading bay and took off.

Later in the afternoon, Mr. Jack told John to bring the carton to the lab. Inside the container was a system which had overheated and caught fire in the field. It surely looked smoky and damaged. At that time, another order was sitting in the lab, so we put it in the carton and rolled it to the shipping bay. Then a truck picked it up later.

"*I have to wait for a police report on that system before I can decide what to do with it,*" Mr. Jack said.

As my sense of inquisitiveness grew stronger, I walked around that burned system several times a day, wondering what could have started the fire.

One day, Mr. Jack told Pat to check the system and see whether we could salvage any of the parts. Without thinking or even letting Mr. Jack finish his statement, I jumped out of my seat and told him I could fix the system.

> **Sure, it was not my first time. Ridiculous jumpiness had grabbed me once when I had turned on an electric light in my dark primary school classroom. Like before, it turns out to be a magic moment.**

Anyway, I managed to achieve one thing by my action—I attracted the attention of everybody in the lab. I could see Glen shaking his head.

"*If you get that system to work again,*" John said, "*consider yourself an engineer.*"

A few hours passed, and then Mr. Jack wanted to know if I was serious about fixing the system.

"*Yes, sir, I am serious,*" I replied.

"*OK, that system is all yours,*" he said. "*If you get it to work again, I will put you on the payroll as a permanent employee.*"

I cannot say I was confident of success. However, I drew comfort from the power of fear-of-failure. I went to work on Monday and began by wiping the frame with a cleaning fluid so I could see the system inside and outside clearly. Then I extracted the power cabinet, cleaned it up, and put it away. On Tuesday, I removed all the electronic circuit boards and stored them in a bin for visual inspection. Next, I cleaned the empty cabinet and let everything dry for a couple of days. Then I inspected each board and put it away for further testing.

After all that, I tested each board and labeled it "good" if it passed and "bad" if it failed. By the time I had tested half of the boards, I had found the board that caused the fire. I put it aside and continued to check the rest. It took me a few weeks to test all the boards and determine how much damage the fire did to the system.

The fire had started in that board and went up to the angle iron along with the wiring. So it took me two weeks to disconnect and remove all the wires and two more weeks to rewire the frame. Then I conducted a thorough safety test after which the system passed the test. With only three weeks left before the end of my co-op period, I put the power cabinet back in the frame and conducted another test with the power supply in operation. Then I replaced the burnt board with a new one.

One week before my co-op ended, I repopulated the rack with the original boards and one new board. As the memory of this once-smoked-system exerted fear and reluctance on me, I turned the system on with my sluggish hands still resisting. But how dare I speak of fear, when it was me who wanted to repair the system. Luckily, it did not smoke. So I let it idle for two hours and then I ran the final test for three hours. On Monday, the happy me informed Mr. Jack the system was working again and handed it over to him. Then he let John test the system for eight hours. Then on Tuesday morning, he gave Mr. Jack the test result and then we met later in his office and enjoyed Pepsi-Cola and cookies.

The president of TeleAudit, Mr. Keagan, was back in the office from his European trip. And he hadn't heard about the system I had repaired. Soon after lunch, we met in his office—to chat about the system and Spectrametrics, a new company in Andover where Jimmy and Tim were working on a computer design project. Then Mr. Jack invited me to his office and gave me the company ID tag, the address, and telephone number of Spectrametrics in Andover, Massachusetts, and informed me I could go to work there any time I don't have classes.

"You're now on my payroll as an engineer," he said.

I realized that I would never come back to TeleAudit on co-op; that

THE AUDACITY OF DESTINY

was it. Nevertheless, I was leaving on friendly terms, and I would always be a welcome visitor—a feeling that got me happy and flying once I got in my car.

For me, though, the co-op had been a huge success. Sure, I do not claim to be smart because I'm not. But I could not think of many other students who were walking around with a company's ID tag, and already employed as an engineer going into their senior year. However, by all accounts, I'd applied myself well enough to earn the recognition of my co-op employer.

Not much was happening during the first week of classes. So on Tuesday, I went to Andover to checkout Spectrametrics and Jimmy and Tim's project. I drove around for a while in Andover and found Spectrametrics at last. But Jimmy and Tim were not in the lab. But their engineering aide, Russ, was there, looking at a large sheet of paper. So I introduced myself to Russ, and then I asked him when Jimmy and Tim come to work.

"They come in when they choose. Some days they work at their home offices," he said. *"You can start by looking through the schematics over there. That's what you will be working on, I guess."*

On Thursday. Tim was in the laboratory drawing schematics, and Russ was separating electronic parts when I arrived at the office. Tim had completed four pages of drawings with two more to go. Sure, I had some familiarity with the art of schematic illustration. But the shit I was looking at—the symbols in his drawings were way over my head. So a sense of inadequacy and self-doubt set in—a natural feeling for someone still in college who hadn't accrued any high-performance expectations.

Meanwhile, the electronic revolution was underway; the electronic vacuum tubes—diodes, triodes, and so on—manufactured by Raytheon, Western Electric, and others were fading away and replaced by chips, ICs, semiconductors, and transistors manufactured by Fairchild, Motorola, and Sony, which had introduced transistor radios already.

To avail myself of the opportunity my co-op employer offered me; I chose my classes so I could go to work a few hours a week. So one day, I arrived at work in the afternoon, and saw a big sign *'DANGER DO NOT ENTER`* on the door next to the lab and Coaxial cable hugging the rug along the hallway to the entrance. I had taken advanced courses on field theory by then, so that configuration seemed at odds with the textbook.

I recall one day, Tim had set up a workbench with two high chairs on both sides. He sat on one with a perforated board, a roll of thin wire, and a few tools on the bench. Then he gave me two drawings. The first was of a board with parts placed on one side, and the second, the reverse side of the same board, with cobwebs of wires twisted on tiny pegs Tim described as wire-wrap.

"Take your time and learn how I arranged the parts," he said.

So I studied the drawings and grasped only one distinctive feature—a large socket he placed at the center had smaller parts around it. But I could not tell why that was the case nor whether they were in any order. Nevertheless, I continued to study the layout, as Tim called it for two days before he invited me to the workbench again and explained it. Then he placed the central piece—the socket on the perforated board first and the others around it. Watching Tim, I noticed that he had placed each chip close to other chips connected to it. I also noticed that the chips had markings on one end. When Tim finished the placement, he took the assembly drawing from me and compared it with his work.

"What do you think?" he inquired.

"They look alike," I said.

"Cut another perforated board of the same dimension like this," Tim instructed as he continued to compare his work with the assembly drawing.

So I cut the piece, filed the edges down, and measured it twice before handing it to Tim. Meanwhile, Spectrametrics had hired three chemists, who walked around like doctors in white robes and white gloves. They had their lab connected to the room with the danger sign on the door. One day, Mr. Keagan came to the lab with a huge man Dr. Douglas and introduced him to Jim. Dr. Douglas was a professor at a university in North Dakota and was working on the atomic emission

THE AUDACITY OF DESTINY

spectrometer.

A Test Of Character

One early Saturday morning, a loud fire truck siren blaring outside my apartment building woke me up. I looked outside and saw a crowd gathering in front of the building. Then I saw smoke entering my apartment from the hallway. For this reason, I put my clothes on in a hurry and threw two trunks in which I had my precious belongings out of the window. Then I jumped down from the second floor into the dumpster and got out with minor cuts and bruises, and then I moved my trunks to Rex and Shegu's apartment. Then we watched the fire consume the entire building from the second floor to the third floor—I lost all my clothes, books, TV, and my radio too.

After the fire, Red Cross representatives collected the names of the occupants of the building and told us where to go for help. Then I moved in with my friends, Rex and Shegu. And I stayed with them until I found another apartment to stay. On Monday, I reported to the office of the Dean of International Students and explained my situation to him. So his office helped me to apply for a work permit. A few weeks later, I got a work permit from the immigration office. I will never forget how sad and hopeless people looked when I went to the Red Cross office, where they were processing the fire victims.

"Do you have a police report?" the lady asked.

"Yes, I do," I replied and gave her the report.

The lady made a copy of my police report and cut me a check for two thousand five hundred dollars without making any demands.

"*This check will help you in small ways to rent another apartment,*" she said.

Suddenly, memory's power—the most reliable counsel in currency when a decision about right and wrong is urgent—reminded me of the fantastic work the Red Cross had done in Nigeria during the Nigeria-Biafra war. So I rejected the check to preserve my personal belief regarding empathy for those who deserve it the most.

Chuks I. Ndukwe

I firmly believe that people who cannot help themselves deserve sincere empathy.

After all, I had been granted a work permit by the immigration department, and I was staying with my friends. In my judgment, I was in a far better condition, and I was not helpless—Indeed, I did not deserve the check. I continued to go to work, where I learned how to wire a computer board—a process called "breadboarding." After my final examination, I had a meeting with Mr. Keagan; I believe the purpose was to reassure me he'd adjust my salary to reflect the prevailing rate for students graduating at the time.

Here's one reason not to be flippant: as Russ and I were leaving the office on Friday, we stopped to chat in the hallway about the cable running along with the rug when I said to him:

"Doug is generating radio frequency, thereby causing the computers inside the lab to whine when he is working in his lab. And running cable on the rug along the hallway is not right either."

During this conversation, I forgot that the saying "walls have ears."

"You can't say that, because you don't know what he is doing in there," Russ said. *"You are right,"* I replied *"but I still think he's not doing the right thing; he's messing with our computers.*

So the last memorable thing I did before my graduation on June 15, 1980, was to opine on Professor Douglas' science project. In other words, I put my foot in my mouth.

Chapter 10

THE AUDACITY OF DESTINY

Being A Scientist

The most confused we ever get is when we're trying to convince our heads of something our heart knows is a lie.

~ Karen Marie Moning

Chuks I. Ndukwe

Job Lends Credence

The reason I talk to myself is because I'm the only one whose answers I accept.

~ George Carlin

On Friday, one week after my graduation, I met Mr. Keagan in his office again for a short meeting. There, we spent the time talking about my foot-in-mouth flippant criticism of Doug's science project. *"I heard your comments on Doug's work,"* he said. *"Tell me why you think he is not doing the right thing."* *"Running wire down the hallway on top of the rug as a grounding scheme, seems a bit odd,"* I answered.

Doug has a PhD in electrical engineering. And the president of PlasmaTherm Inc.—a company in Pennsylvania that manufactures the atomic plasma emission power supply Spectrametrics intended to use to power its spectrometer had recommended to work on their system. He had been at it for six months, and hasn't done jack! Moreover, the effect of whatever he's doing in his lab was causing computers in the engineering lab to whine every time he turned his system on.

> **Doug's problem was the same even for medical doctors—the side effect of the medicine they prescribe—not necessarily a flawed diagnostics or mental deficiency.**

The following Monday, I came to work and heard that Doug had left. I feared I might have had a part to play in that—so what! I'd only told the truth. The first time I saw what Doug was working on, I had just entered the lab with Mr. Keagan. Then he walked around the system and stood at the center of the lab.

"This is the atomic plasma emission power supply," he said. *"I want you to take over the project. Don't be afraid; I will give you any assistance you need."*

A Defining Moment

My first reaction was recalling the question I had asked Mr. David Marshal back in my primary school classroom. *"Is every electrical engineer, a scientist?"*

> **What burns me about a lie is not the lie. It's that I am too trusting of the liar to accept the lie.**

Although his answer was in the affirmative, I knew it was this project—my first after graduating from college—that would confirm the answer Mr. David Marshal had given in a personal, practical and believable fashion. Shortly after lunch, a memo went out to inform the employees that Doug had left the company and I'd be taking over the project.

"Chuks, I think Mr. Keagan heard you the other day," Russ said.

"It's odd for a fresh college graduate to take on such a project," Tim said. *"I am glad that you've finished breadboarding your computer board so I can spare you for some time."*

After that, I rushed to Northeastern University library to research atomic plasma emission but found nothing relevant there. I checked the company's library—nothing there either. Seven days later, I was still a mile away from figuring out what to do or how to start. Then came my self-condemnation for speaking out about Doug's work. However, despite this shaky start, my rattled mind held on to the eternal hope—embedded in the truth—success comes to those who persevere. So I stripped down everything Doug did.

The first week ended with me still clueless about how to start. I felt funny, like a touch of flu-like nervousness. However, the fear of failure and a real shame I'd feel from ridicule kept refilling the cup of will—my mind fed itself. After all, isn't science; knowledge attained through study and practice, or simply messing with the unfamiliar?

> **Confidence is difficult to come by in certain situations such as the one I was in with nothing to grab on to—still hope prevailed over fear.**

On Monday, I faked cool and began to clean the room. I opened every piece of paper—looking for something even if that thing was still blurry in my thoughts. Maybe I was giving my brain time to boot up.

Surprisingly, I found a plastic wrap taped to the chimney on top of the system—***the atomic plasma emission product specification,*** which appeared to be the clue I desperately needed. *"The system tends to be noisy,"* the document noted. *"It is to be deployed in a quiet room."*

The term ***quiet room*** hit me like a brick, so I went after it. I found nothing electrical; different books and journals described it in terms of suppression of noise or echo in the room. "You can achieve it with a specific wall, ceiling, and floor types," they claim. So I abandoned the research quickly and almost quit the job.

> **But memory is like a firecracker; a single tiny flame can shine a light on one small lost glittery ornament in a mountain of dust.**

Suddenly it happened: tugged out of the slough of despair, I remembered one simple thing I did at the Nigerian petroleum refinery that had produced a profound result—repairing the grounding scheme of the control panel. When I'd finished, all the static noise went away. *"It has to be the same technique,"* I comforted myself thinking.

Amid this confusing thought process, I realized the project would require time and dedication, so I paid the lady who was babysitting my daughters, Ere and Ugo, for additional two hours so I could work late.

One valuable thing I did during this uncertain period was to write a project plan. So I finished it and gave it to Mr. Keagan and continued to scan the *Yellow Pages* in search of the parts I needed for the project. Mr. Keagan read the plan and came to the lab to express his delight saying, *"Mr. Professor did his job without a plan."*

THE AUDACITY OF DESTINY

Who can blame Doug? Professors do not go by project plans. They synthesize theories and deliver the material with authority. But the practice is a bit unforgiving and leaves nothing for pedantry.

"Sir, I just want to give you the idea of what I'll be doing in the coming weeks," I said. *"It looks like a plan,"* he replied.

At this time, my fear had begun to recede as my confidence re-emerged and asserted itself. I went to work on Saturday with a renewed sense of optimism. I had a cup of tea and began to measure the distance from the shallow lake that ran behind the building to the outside wall of the lab where the company deployed the system. Then Mr. Keagan arrived and came over to the shallow lakeside and watched me for a while.

"You haven't told me how much the project will cost," he said. *"I've bought everything I need already,"* I replied. *"What did you buy?"* he questioned. *"I bought a four feet copper rod; a hundred-feet roll of three-inch-wide copper strip, a soldering iron, flux, and solder."*

"Do you have the receipt?" He asked.

"Yes, sir, it is inside the lab."

"Put the receipt on my desk," he said. *"Anytime you buy anything, including lunch, or dinner during nonworking hours, I want you to give me the receipt."*

I terminated the copper strip on the copper rod, drove it into the ground at the waterside, and dug up a trench from the waterside to the building. Next, I threaded the strip through a pipe I had buried in the ditch. Then I dragged the piece up the wall, through the ceiling, into the room, and finally, I bolted the strip to the base of the system. After visual inspections and testing with instruments, I discovered that most of the metallic parts and electrical connections were seated on paint, thereby making partial or no metallic contact with each other. Indeed, I had made a significant discovery—the cause of the static noise.

Once I made this dramatic discovery, it took me two months to disconnect the parts, scrape the paint off, and reconnect the pieces. The system had been off for some time now, so nobody remembered the frustration of watching computers whine and freeze up when Doug powered the system up.

On Friday, Tim asked Russ to come to work on Saturday to help him, so I came to work as well. While Tim was working on his computer, I turned the atomic plasma emission power supply on and ambled to the engineering lab afraid that Tim would yell or scream at me, but nobody screamed.

Then came sudden self-awareness that I was close to success where Doug had failed. So the temptation to gloat almost forced a few bragging words out of me but I resisted it and recognized my limitations—the yet-to-get-off-the-ground state of my professional life. After that, a cool head prevailed. Instead of celebrating about it, I sat with Tim in the lab until closing time. The following week, out of curiosity, I drew a circle around the system and divided it into six equal sections of 60 degrees.

> **Of course, I was trying to verify what I had read once in a textbook—that radio-frequency interference radiates in an isotropic pattern—in every direction.**

One day, when the office had closed, and the workers had gone home, I began to rotate the system in 60-degree increments through 360 degrees. At each point, I turned the system off and on, and the computers worked without whining. Then I disconnected the copper strip and separated the joints with plastic sheets and repeated the exercise. Each time I turned the system off and on, the computers whined and crashed just as they did when Doug worked on the project. Then I removed the plastic sheets and reconnected the parts and the copper strip to the system and then it worked flawlessly again.

THE AUDACITY OF DESTINY

People's act of kindness had brought tears to my eyes many times before. But this time—alone in the lab, I find tears flowing down my cheeks for a different reason—the force of sheer humility. I had accomplished the task Doug failed at, and it's not fair; he's more deserving of the success than me.

Eventually, I collected myself and spent another month on the project report; it was my first, so I described everything I did systematically before, during, and after the completion of the project. Finally, I showed Mr. Keagan how the system was working and gave him the project report, which he read and made a few changes.

On the following Monday, the executive staff discussed the project report in their weekly meeting, after which Mr. Keagan sent for me. *"Could you give us a quick demo of what you've written in this report?"* Mr. Keagan asked. *"And what you referred to as isotropic radiation."*

I opened the research lab and excused myself to visit the men's room as the staff gathered around the system. You could have guessed it, I was nervous and needed a deep breath. Now with all the computers turned on and employees are working on their computers as usual. I demonstrated what I had written in the report, and none of the machines whined.

After the demonstration, Mr. Keagan sent a copy to Mr. Block, the president of PlasmaTherm—the manufacturer of the atomic plasma emission power supply. A few weeks later, Mr. Keagan received a reply from Mr. Block. It was a blistering condemnation of my report, which he described as "nonsense."

Mr. Keagan called me to his office and read the letter to me and added, *"I will invite Mr. Block over with his chief scientific officer, and we will have you do a demonstration for us in our conference room. What do you think about that?"*

"That will be fine," I replied.

"Is three weeks enough time to get the conference room ready?" he

asked.

"Yes, I believe so, sir," I replied.

As the big day got closer, the butterflies in my stomach flew hither and thither with increasing intensity. In the meantime, I got a nice haircut and had my black suit dry-cleaned. I also sought advice from Jimmy. Then he told me a story about his first public speech; how his throat had dried up and his voice faded, and he coughed his ass off.

"You have done the work already," he said. *"Follow your project report page by page. I read it, and I can tell you it is pretty good. Keep a cup of water or tea by your side."*

A few days before the demonstration, we received one system from PlasmaTherm and then Russ, and I moved it to the conference room and let it sit in one corner of the room.

On a momentous day, the guests arrived as I was helping Tim to debug my breadboard. Then Mr. Keagan showed them around and introduced them to Jimmy. At nine o'clock, Jimmy joined them for the initial one-hour meeting before I joined them in the conference room.

"This is my new engineer, who took over the project from Douglas," Mr. Keagan said. *"His name is Chuks I. Ndukwe, he graduated from Northeastern University six months ago, and he is here to demonstrate his work for us."*

So I went from page to page of my report and described what I had done and why. When I got to the final test, I asked the people at the computer stands to report any computer malfunction during the demonstration. Then I turned the system on—and there were no complaints! I turned it off, and there were no complaints either. I turned to the page where I had described the radio frequency radiated by the system as isotropic. Then I showed them the mapping on the floor and rotated the system through 360 degrees in 60-degree increments. At every point, I turned the system off, waited for one minute, and then I turned it on again; the system behaved the same, and the computers did not whine.

"This concludes part one of the demonstration," I said.

"Let's take a break. We will continue after lunch," Mr. Keagan said.

During lunch, I moved the system to the corner and replaced it with the system we had just received from PlasmaTherm. Then after lunch, I went back to the conference room and continued part two of the demonstration.

"This system came to us from the manufacturer as you see it," I said.

I turned the system on, and all the computers whined and crashed. I proceeded to rotate the system in the same manner that I tested the first system; then I told them that "In effect what I did was to shield or suppress the radiation from the system."

After the demonstration, Plasma Therm's chief scientific officer, Mr. Gross, invited me to their office in Mount Laurel to speak with his development staff.

At the end of the year, PerkinElmer—a company located in California, if my memory of it is not mistaken—bought Spectrametrics, so I got laid off.

Chapter 11

THE AUDACITY OF DESTINY

Pride and Rivalry

It is best to keep one's own state intact; to crush the enemy's state is only second best.

~ Sun Tzu

THE AUDACITY OF DESTINY

Order and Logic

Reason itself is fallible, and this fallibility must find a place in our logic.

~Nicola Abbagnano

Everybody has something he'll never outgrow or purge from his mind. Mine is a phenomenon in software engineering—coding a concept, compiling the program, and running it, only to find the result wrong owing to faulty order, logic, or the improper initialization of variables. Each time I wander into this obscure terrain of thought, I'd see a big sign "order" and "logic" flashing in my mind: sequencing in terms of position, value, space, time, and importance; occurring in a fixed definable place; the number of times differentiation applied successively—to anchor my passion for software coding and computer science in general.

So I had gone back to school to continue my studies in computer science and started a part-time job with Codex Corporation in Stoughton, Massachusetts. The company manufactured modems used to interconnect computers before the advent of the Internet. There were a few fresh college graduates and engineers from Northeastern University, Lowell University, MIT, the University of Massachusetts, Pen State, and others in my department.

My assignment was to design and code a program to recognize the Bundespost (the German telephone and telegraph regulatory agency) ring signal. I shared a cubicle with an electrical engineer, Larry J. He worked on hardware, things like PCB, ICs, chips, and sockets, and I wrote software. Every country has PTT (postal, telephone, and telegraph) regulations, and each agency must test and approve every telecommunication product sold in that country.

Chuks I. Ndukwe

We were grabbing cups of coffee, tea and toast in the cafeteria for breakfast one brisk summer morning when the chilling news broke that *"Codex's modem had failed an agency approval test in the United Kingdom."* Everything froze, and the ringing voices faded.

Then the hardware engineering manager, Mr. John M. called an emergency meeting immediately and gave the official version; *"Our modem failed agency test in the United Kingdom this morning,"* he said. *"But we still have three hours to make changes and get it to pass."*

"What parameters did it fail?" Pete asked.

"The ring detector came on too fast," John, answered. *"I want all of you to come up with a solution before you leave this conference room."* Then he locked us up.

We were racing against time, so the scramble for a solution began immediately. For the caliber of engineers in the department, the answer should be easy. It seemed as though a group of fresh graduates from different universities passionate about the prestige of their alma mater would coalesce around a single technical solution, but that notion proved to be flawed.

The discussion quickly turned into a struggle for academic superiority. Each person offered equations and ideas, some of which were impractical and others that would take days, if not weeks, to implement. I listened to their arguments and wondered how confident they were in their ideas or knew the technical details in the first place.

> **It's at times like this that the quality of each institution's system of education and not the instruction or instructors is tested. For me, Northeastern was under test.**

But I was a software engineer—an outsider looking in. It was a hardware issue, totally outside my purview. So I could stay quiet — except that would make me appear dumb. Then I realized that if I came

THE AUDACITY OF DESTINY

up with the solution, I'd be revered in the department, if not companywide. Still, I was an F1 student on a part-time, with little to gain in the saga.

However, when the electrical engineers failed to reach a consensus, the meeting adjourned. Then I borrowed the modem drawing and the UK ring-detector requirement from Larry and studied them for about thirty minutes. Then I attached one resistor and one capacitor to the ring detector circuitry—after I'd calculated its rise time or time delay (a simple scheme from a simple mathematical model). Then I evaluated it in the lab, and the modem passed the test.

So the manager called the United Kingdom and told the Codex representative what to do. In less than two hours, the news came back that "the modem had passed the test." Then my name spread like wildfire.

> **In the final analysis, I believe it is this simple scheme—a resistor and a capacitor—that launched my professional career in the United States.**

The following Monday morning, John opined about an AT&T telephone interface in a meeting and how they used a coil in the interface to loop direct current back to the central office.

"We'd like to reduce the size of the modem," he said. *"But it is impossible as long as we continue to use the coil."*

He called for a volunteer to look into ways of replacing the coil with a smaller active device. *"The size of our modems are too large for our customer's liking,"* he stressed.

In the next weekly meeting, he again stressed the importance and urgency of the project. Now, he kept looking at me as if to say *"come on man you can do this."* So that action-spurring sense of urgency everybody hazes goes to work, and as my inner-voice got inaudibly louder, my inner-guide compelled me to volunteer. So I told John I'd like to try if I had enough time to devote to the project.

"See me after the meeting," he replied.

Chuks I. Ndukwe

Before I went to see John, I'd met his boss, and got the message that they'd hire me full time and pay my tuition fees if I agreed to work on the project full time and go to school part-time.

I began the work of modifying the AT&T telephone interface; I came up with a schematic diagram of the new interface and showed it to John, expecting compliments. But he did not disparage nor compliment me—instead, he said,
"The general concept looks OK, but the part you selected is suspect. Find another active device that will do the same job."

One day, I tried one of the parts, a field-effect transistor, or FET, I had selected; surprise, surprise—it went up in flames, and everybody in the lab cheered as the smoke rose to the ceiling. Then I tried another power transistor a week later, and that too, overheated and blew up.

However, it's those initial failures that revealed to me the very critical aspect of electronic product design and engineering; 'component's characteristics and functional specifications.' Now I discovered that the characteristics of the device I had selected were incompatible with the function for which I needed it, not necessarily the concept itself, so I went back to the proverbial drawing board.

Once during lunch break, when I bumped into John in the hallway on his way back from the cafeteria, he asked how my project was going.

"I've fused up the two transistors I selected, and I'm searching for a different type," I said.

Then he gave me a catalogue of transistors and asked me to look through the section captioned *"Darlington Array Transistors."* I spent a few days studying the description, different configurations of the Darlington array and their characteristics. Then I made my selection after reading up on their specifications and limitations. I tried one of the arrangements—hello! It worked without blowing up. Then I tried different combinations until I found a set that met the current requirements and demonstrated it to John.

THE AUDACITY OF DESTINY

"We are not there yet," he said. *"We have to replace the hybrid transformer to reduce the interface to the desired size."*

But I had no idea where to find a miniature transformer. So I looked through different catalogues and publications until my eyes almost dropped off their sockets. It became apparent the project was not at all trivial. Of course, if it were, somebody would have done it earlier.

One day, John came to my cubicle with a guest, Mr. Siegel, a representative of a miniature transformer manufacturer in the UK. He told me they'd make a custom transformer for me if I gave him its specifications. So I gave it to him and had lunch with him before he left.

A few weeks later, I offered two design proposals: one for a generic telephone interface and another *DAA* (direct-access arrangement). After reviewing the projects, the management approved both concepts, so I began the design.

Two months later, I completed the design. And handed it over to K. Miller and continued with my software design. I can't say I know why, but I withheld the DAA design. It's the only thing unique in my toy box. A few months later, in the weekly meeting, John announced that he had submitted the skinny modem with my interface and ring-signal-detection software in it for approval in Germany—where getting modem approval is most difficult. And my anxiety level went off the chart.

On Friday—the day of the approval, we waited for news from Germany until lunchtime. We began to speculate that the test did not go well despite the differences in the time zone. For me, though, the old saying *"No news is good news"* still held. Suddenly we got the news that "the modem had passed the German Bundespost approval test." Following that update, the company buzzed with jubilation.

I had filed for a green card in 1980, just after my graduation from college, but after several hearings, the Department of Immigration and Naturalization services denied my application. Then my lawyer appealed the ruling. The next morning, the Codex's receptionist, Mrs. Ester Forbes, informed me that her husband, Ervin Forbes, a manager at Microcom in Norwood wanted to see me. *"Why does he want to see me?"* I asked. *"I am not sure,"* she answered.

The following day at lunchtime, I met Mr. Forbes in his office at Microcom for a short meeting we spent discussing the news of Codex's modem approvals in Europe and how I'd help Microcom get their modems approved. Sensing my unwillingness to say much, he invited me back. Then on my way home, I met Mr. Forbes again. This time he gave me the modem on his desk and the schematic and asked me whether it was good enough for approval in any European country, but I could not offer any advice knowing I surely was not an expert in the field.

"This is the deal," he said. *"We are willing to do all we can to bring you over to Microcom."* Then he conferred with his boss, Mr. Sauka, the director. At the end of our meeting, they offered me attractive direct and fringe benefits, including filing immigrant visa application on my behalf.

"I have to talk with my attorney about that," I said before leaving.

Then I went home, called my attorney, Mr. Silverson, and told him what Mr. Forbes had told me.

"It sounds like a wonderful idea. Do you understand the kind of visa they are talking about?" he asked.

"No, I don't."

"It's the kind of visa reserved for foreigners who are coming to this country with exceptional technical ability," he said. "*That means the company is having difficulty finding Americans to do the job they want you to do for them. Give my number to Mr. Forbes and have him call me."*

One day, attorney Silverson called me, and during our telephone conversation, he informed me he had discussions with both Mr. Forbes and Sauka.

"We are moving ahead with the filing of your immigrant visa," he said *"We will do that and wait for the outcome of the appeal on your original application. So feel free to join them."*

With that encouragement in mind, I called Mr. Forbes the following day and accepted his offer. Then on Friday, I submitted my

THE AUDACITY OF DESTINY

two weeks' notice to John, my manager.

On July 20, 1987, I reported for work at Microcom, Norwood, Massachusetts, next town over from Roslindale, where I lived. I met with Mr. Peterson, the human resources manager and filled out employment forms. Then Mr. Forbes introduced me around as the international product development engineer.

He'd split the lab and dedicated a section—one-man-lab for the international products development. Six months later, I completed Microcom's first global modem with my DAA interface. Then Microcom's European sales representative, Martin, who lived in Sydney, Australia, took the modem to the United Kingdom, and obtained approval.

Martin arrived at Microcom and announced the passage of the approval test in the UK. Then the company went into a celebratory frenzy. In a short meeting we had with Martin, he indicated he observed something unique in the DAA design and asked me to explain it. I spread the schematic on the table and explained how the modem connects virtually to the central telephone office, even in idle mode—waiting for a ring signal. *"That's why I called it direct-access arrangement,"* I said.

"We can provision the central office system to send the name and number of the call originator while the modem is ringing," Martin said.

I did not see that coming, and Mr. Forbes was taken aback at the idea. *"Ervin, this is a brilliant design,"* he said. *"I can make lots of money selling this feature alone. Figure out how to get the modem to display the incoming data."*

One evening, attorney Silverson called and told me to get ready to travel to Nigeria for the processing of my immigrant visa. *"Your background check is complete,"* he said.

Then In March 1990, I received a letter from the Immigration office giving me a date to report to the American embassy in Lagos,

Chuks I. Ndukwe

Nigeria, with the documents listed in the message. So I traveled to Nigeria on August 7, 1990. On August 10, 1990, I went through the interview successfully, did my health screening and vaccinations and returned to the United States.

Arriving at the JFK International Airport in New York on a blistering summer day, August 14, 1990, I received my visa. Then I called my attorney and informed him my trip was successful.

"Guess what," he said. "Your *appeal of the original application was granted as well. Now you have two green cards. Isn't that amazing? Welcome home, my friend.*"

I arrived at work on Monday, August twenty, 1990, with a sense of gratitude, determined to live up to Microcom's expectations—getting their modems approved in every country in Europe. But that expectation would not last. In January 1991, the owner of Microcom sold the company to Multitech—another modem company I had not heard of before. So I got laid off.

One day in winter, February 1991, I was still collecting my unemployment checks when Mr. McCarthy, vice president at USRobotics in Skokie, Illinois, called and invited me for an interview. On Monday, February eleven, Mr. McCarthy began the meeting by telling me about his company and the international telecom expo that would start in a few weeks in Hanover, Germany.

"*I came back from Germany just to chat with you,*" he said. "*When I was there making preparations for the Expo, your name came up quite a bit. Is it true you got modems approved for Codex and Microcom in the United Kingdom and Germany?*"

"*That's true, sir,*" I said.

After the interview, Mr. McCarthy made me an offer that was much more than I had expected. For that reason, and because I was a job seeker, I accepted his offer.

"*When are you starting?*" he asked. "*I need you here ASAP.*"

"I'd like to start on Monday, February 18," I said.

"All right, I'll have a moving company arrange for your relocation," he said. "See you then."

THE AUDACITY OF DESTINY

Finally, the moving company arrived in Brockton on February sixteen and loaded my belongings in the truck, including my car. Then I left Brockton on February seventeen and arrived in Chicago in the evening.

Chapter 12

THE AUDACITY OF DESTINY

All Set To Go

Try not to become a man of success. Rather become a man of value.

~ Albert Einstein

THE AUDACITY OF DESTINY

Stepping Out

Success is not final, failure is not fatal: it is the courage to continue that counts.

~ Winston S. Churchill

I arrived at USRobotics in Skokie, Illinois on February 18, 1991, believing that one day, people's perception of me would become real—but that would happen only when there was substance, experience, and résumé to show for it. The company had arranged for me to stay in a private house, a "bed and breakfast" in Evanston, Illinois, until I found an apartment.

On my first day at work, I got my first assignment—to review USRobotics' international products and report back in two days. Mr. McCarthy wanted to know why the company's products were failing approvals in Europe. So he dropped off two modems in my office—a Courier and a Sportster.

Reviewing the modems—engineers blunder in that instant—I noticed zinc-coated cardboard covering the radiative section of the modem I'd correct later. By the end, I had sketched up a brilliant corrective version in my mind and reported to Mr. McCarthy the following day.

During this review period, I'd sometimes implant a few facts—I'd give my would-be critics—a hard nut to crack, and even let them carry it around and try nervously.

"Is there anything we can do to comply with the international modem requirements?" The VP of engineering asked. I faked restraint but alluded to the difficulty of getting substandard products approved in Europe. A few days later, Mr. McCarthy gave me a plane ticket and told

me he would pick me up at Frankfurt Airport in Germany on my arrival there.

The following day, I found a vacant apartment at 169 Ridge Avenue in Chicago for which the company paid the security deposit and the first monthly rent. Then I gave Mr. McCarthy's secretary, Miss Gavana, the key to the apartment so the maintenance people could move my belongings in should the moving truck arrive in my absence.

On my arrival at Frankfurt Airport on Sunday, March 3, at ten o'clock in the morning, Mr. McCarthy picked me up and drove directly to the CeBIT—the International Telecommunication Exposition in Hanover. We walked straight to the USRobotics' booth where he introduced me to the crew, showed me around the expo, and returned to the United States. A few days later, Miss Gavana joined the team.

The expo was a magnificent as every country showed off her best in telecommunication engineering. American companies—AT&T, Motorola, USRobotics, and others featured prominently. I remember trying to visit all the telecom booths in the complex. I walked around all day and staggered back with achy feet; that's how large it was. The following day, I visited every country's postal, telephone, and telegraph (PTT) departments, registered my name in their visitor logbooks, and requested copies of their rules and regulations. It was my Halloween night—trick or treat! So I visited most modem manufacturers, played with their modems, and grabbed their product specifications to see what they were up to. Then I returned to the United States on Sunday, March 17, compiled my trip report after recovering from the jet lag, and gave it to Mr. McCarthy to his utter surprise and appreciation.

I arrived at work on Monday morning a little late because my belongings had arrived while I was in Germany and I had not sorted things out yet. Entering the building, the receptionist, Miss Howard, and a few other employees greeted me with congratulations that came out of nowhere. I logged into my computer that morning, read the memo from Mr. McCarthy, and learned he had promoted me to the manager of the international research and development department. Like the sound of a gunshot, you'd hear walking home in a quiet and safe neighborhood, the

THE AUDACITY OF DESTINY

notice of my promotion was that sudden. So I tried but failed to escape self-doubt. I must confess; I was overwhelmed by emotions, so I did the only thing a reasonable person would do—seek God's guide. After all, it's in moments like this that our inner-guide does its best through the inner-voice as in this case by reminding me that I had supervised a group of people before; this recall shored up my belief and philosophy about people supervision:

> **I believe that managing workers is the art of empowering and inspiring people to do what is expected of them to their fullest potential without unnecessary pressure.**

I never met the manager I replaced. But I'd heard he traveled to Sweden to repair a modem but never came back to his office. His backpack, shoes, and tie remained scattered around the office and grabbed my attention every time I walked into my office. How obscene it was managing the department I had criticized for their lack of diligence and technical rigor! Worse than the professional was the emotional aspect—which was replacing their manager, probably a friend they've had for years.

Still, I was hired to do the job right, and nothing mattered more than doing the job to the company's expectation and making the management proud. At this time, you can imagine how my promotion was received. I'd spend the first-week meeting with my engineers face-to-face, on a one-on-one basis, to lay out my philosophy on the job the company expected us to do.

On Monday, I had my first weekly department meeting. So I posted the mission statement I'd written and handed a copy to each engineer. Soon after, just before the meeting started, Mr. McCarthy joined the meeting and grabbed a copy too. The mission statement read something like this:

> **The International Research and Development Department of USRobotics will strive to be the best in the industry by designing, developing,**

and releasing quality products on a timely basis. Getting approval in every country and meeting the company's time-to-market objectives.

Then we spent most the time discussing how it feels when a modem fails approval testing and the exhilaration when it passes. In that instant, I told my engineers how I felt the first time my design passed approval tests in the United Kingdom and Germany. And I believe it was that telling that changed their minds about me because they've neither seen nor heard from anybody—in person who'd gotten modems approved in both countries before.

Before Mr. McCarthy left the meeting, he invited me to his office one hour before lunch. There we chatted about my observations and plans to redesign the entire company's international products. *"Let's go to lunch,"* he said suddenly.

So we went to Mama Leona, an Italian joint renowned for its lasagna, and spent two hours going over my trip report, especially my observations about a portfolio of pocket-size and palm-top modems made by another company, Worldport. *"I'm in negotiations to acquire that company,"* John said. Then after lunch, he gave me a check for five thousand dollars on our way back to work. *"This ought to last till you get paid in two weeks,"* he said.

So I opened a bank account in Chicago with that check thinking; I might make it after all.

Easing The Ire

At my next weekly meeting, I distributed schedules for approvals in the United Kingdom, Germany, France, and Australia. Then I invited my engineers to choose the project they'd like to work on from the list.

I must say, it was this concept of choice rather than I assignment—the idea of letting the engineers choose what they'd like to work on—rather than a direct appointment to their projects by the manager, that unleashed their potential and dedication to their projects. They owned their projects, leaving me free only to guide and provide algorithms when necessary.

THE AUDACITY OF DESTINY

One day, four months later, John stopped by my office to chat and expressed satisfaction in my engineers' change of attitude. I'd realize that what he came for was to find out the status of our projects. So I gave it to him—I informed him I'd travel to Aurora next week for emission and safety tests after which the modems would be ready for approval testing. The following week, I released the modems for approval tests in the United Kingdom and Germany.

On Monday morning, John came to my office with a gentleman; he had a smile on his face as they walked into my office. He had a familiar face, but I'd forgotten his name. Let me confess; I have a giant vacuum in my mind for names and events like birthdays, wedding and other anniversaries. And I'm still paying a heavy price for it. So John reintroduced us, and then I remembered: we'd met once at Microcom and his name was Martin Franklin. Martin and I embraced each other. Then we chatted about his trip to the UK and Germany and later, I handed him all the documents he needed for his journey.

"How far have you gone with that INI stuff?" Martin asked. *"It's been on my mind since I spoke to you last at Microcom."*

"Chuks, this is the man who told me to go after you when I was in Germany," John said. *"And I can tell you he is happy you're here."*

Martin wanted the INI feature in his Australian modem. *"The central telephone office in Sydney is ready to make an allowance for its provisioning,"* he said.

"What is, INI?" John asked.

"That's the feature I told you Chuks invented at Microcom before they sold the company: incoming-number identification," he said. *"It allows the modem to receive data like the number and name of the call originator during the ringing period and display the information on the screen for the call receiver to see."*

"Are you sure?" John inquired.

"Yes, we can sell this feature as caller ID," Martin said.

Chuks I. Ndukwe

"What do you need to implement this feature?" John inquired again. *"And how long will it take?"*

"I have completed my part," I said. *"We need the DSP department to get involved so they can answer that question."*

So John invited Mike, the DSP department manager, to join us, then I repeated what I said about the feature and what was left to complete its implementation.

"How long will it take to finish it?" John asked again.

Mike recites the litany of the current event-driven displays he had in the modem software, and ended with the usual uncommitted answer managers are known for; *"I would say a matter of weeks or one month in the worst case."*

In the meantime, we've almost completed phase one of the Australian modem development. So after the meeting, I demonstrated its performance for Martin and John in the lab. Then Martin left for the UK.

While it was great, the modems had gone out for testing; it was hard to pretend all would go well and even harder to imagine how devastated my engineers would feel if the modems fail the test.

So there I sat in my office, leg crossed, squeezing my soft rubber ball attempting to hide my fear about the modem failure. I stayed in my office, avoided my people, just played drums with my pencils and desk, and occasionally squeezed my finger-conditioning softball. I had a few flashbacks of how few managers got off quips at my expense when I announced my intention to redesign the international modems. Yes, that's me; I was experiencing the clash of confidence and virtuous insecurity.

It's the longest four days I had ever lived. Then came the day of reckoning! The British Telephone tested the modems on Thursday. Then on Friday, Martin called from London. *"We've got approval in Germany and the UK,"* he said.

THE AUDACITY OF DESTINY

Before I got to the lab, John's memo announcing the approval had hit like a rocket and the company was in a frenzy.

One month later, the DSP department burned EPROM with the *Caller-Id* feature; then I tested it in the engineering lab successfully. When Martin called from Australia, we could see his number and his name on the modem screen. Next, I demonstrated the feature at the DSP lab again to their delight. Finally, I called Martin back and informed him the test was successful. After a few minor modifications, I released the modem for Australian approval. Then a few weeks later, John sent out a memo that Australia had approved our modem.

> **The moment of truth arrived sooner than I anticipated—my engineers' transformation from can't-do to can-do. Loafers to achievers hit me like lightning. As the engineers celebrated, I took comfort in the gratification of mission accomplished.**

But we still had not done the French modem yet. So everybody joined in the French project; you could see three or four engineers staring at the computer screen, pointing at data points and sometimes laughing, and I would not have had it any other way.

> **For me, there's no more fabulous gift a manager can get from the people he manages than the commitment to their work, having fun, and with smiles on their faces while doing the work.**

On October 9, 1991, I boarded a plane for Geneva, Switzerland, and arrived on October 10 to assist USRobotics' crew run the International Telecommunication Exposition. Two of us, Miss Sylvia Gavana and I, had participated in the show before, but it was my first time in Switzerland. So I spent one pleasant week demonstrating USRobotics' modems to visitors—who came to our booth.

At the end of the expo, on October 17, USRobotics held a gala at the hotel ballroom. Mr. Delabie and I were arranging for the next

Chuks I. Ndukwe

modem approval in France, consequently, I missed most of the occasion. So I walked into the hall when the entertainment was almost over, and Martin had already accepted an *USTelecom91* lapel pin on my behalf. He waved me up to the podium and pinned the lapel on my suit. Then he introduced me as "the man behind the Caller ID."

As the fiscal year began to wind down, Mr. McCarthy and my boss Mr. Lange invited me to a product planning meeting he dedicated to allocating money for my department. I had put together my product-development plan for the next fiscal year based on my dream of dominating the international modem market Hayes had dominated in the past. I projected two modem approvals per quarter in every country where USRobotics did business.

Amidst projections, actuals, and allowances for flawed estimation, I accumulated five thousand dollars for my team-building efforts and a total of eight hundred thousand dollars for my projects and travels. And two thousand, five hundred dollars reimbursement for the amount I had spent building my team in the past.

At this moment, my only brother Dick lived in Ghana where he had used clothing business, so I decided to help give his company a jump start. I traveled to Ghana on November 29, 1992, to get a better understanding of the conditions of his business. Then I returned to the United States on December 14, went to work on Monday, and faced a tough decision—a tough choice indeed.

On the one hand, I was happy with my job, but my brother's business lay weary on the other, to say the least; he needed me. Seeing this, I slid down the slippery slope to the tight spot in the mind where I make difficult decisions. And there I became irrelevant and my job trivial. So I had to choose between career and family. In the end, I wanted my family's success more than anything else. I quit and started a used-clothing export business—a conduit for my brother's business. Then I began to ship containers of used clothing to Ghana until the company collapsed under its weight. Consequently, amid eviction order and the foreclosure of my warehouse, I learned one crucial lesson:

THE AUDACITY OF DESTINY

Loss of thousands of dollars on a good cause, especially family matters, hardly lands as much a punch as a nickel overpayment on a loaf of bread.

And there I was one night, as I lay in my bed with a few days left to vacate my apartment. Suddenly a signal—in the form only the inner-power sends, became apparent and compelled me to act. I got up and checked for job openings in the newspaper—in the *Chicago Sun-Times*, I found an opportunity for a senior electrical engineer at ADC Telecommunications in Minnetonka, Minnesota. I emailed my résumé and went back to sleep.

Then the company replied on Monday and invited me for an interview. I arrived at Saint Paul International Airport, under sub-zero temperature, and drove to the hotel in Plymouth, Minnesota, where the company had planned for me to stay for the interview. Then it snowed again that night, and the temperature dropped like a rock down to several degrees below zero. The parking lot was underground and heated. So I had no problem getting out in the morning. Then on my way to ADC, I hit the ramp and had the highway all to myself because there were no cars on the road, and driving was treacherous. Therefore, I crawled at low gear and driving speed to ADC Telecommunications. When I arrived at ADC, the company was closed, and there were only two cars in the parking lot. But surprisingly, the vice president and the hiring manager were in their offices.

After warming up with a steamy cup of tea, we met at the vice president's office for my interview—an amicable one indeed. I knew I got the job when they began to ask how much money I was expecting.

Problem Solver

The day I started work at ADC Telecommunications, 125 White water drive, Minnetonka Minnesota, it snowed all day, and the temperature was a few degrees below zero—which was a lot warmer than the day I had come in for the interview. I settled in my cubicle. The manager, Uma, introduced me around and I grabbed a cup of hot cocoa.

Chuks I. Ndukwe

My title, 'senior engineer' was different from the previous title; since I was a 'manager' then and my cubicle was next to another senior engineer, Mike Wanless.

Without wasting any time, I began to learn about hybrid fiber-coax (HFC) technology and how I'd fit within the larger scheme of things. ADC's HFC system shared some features with the modem technology—the line interface. There, I took comfort—in my familiarity with those shared features, I can shamelessly claim to be as good at as anybody in the telecommunication industry.

A few months later, ADC promoted the manager, Mr. Uma Kamath to a director, and Mike to the manager. When I went over to congratulate Mike after the announcements, he was freaking out. And before I uttered the word "congratulations," he put his finger over my lips and hushed me up.

"I have something to tell you," he said. *"Let's go to the Chinese restaurant."*
"I don't eat Chinese food," *I said. "I think I am allergic to it."*
"OK, how about a steak house?"
"That sounds good," I replied.

When we got to the steak house, he ordered beer, and I ordered Pepsi. Then he began,

"Chuks, I don't want to be a manager," he said. *"I wish Uma had talked to me before making the announcement. You've been a manager before; you should take the job."*

"You're not drunk, are you?" I asked. *"You can't pass up a promotion like that."* So I volunteered to help him in any way he wanted or needed. *"Take the job and pretend to love it,"* I advised. I offered to help prepare his briefings for Monday staff meetings. *"Hang in there. After two to three weeks you will become comfortable,"* I said.

Strange as it were, that chat at the restaurant helped bring us together as the friends we'd become later. Every day after work, we'd spend one hour going over existing technical issues, and I'd volunteer to work on some important ones, like the HFC-system malfunction.

THE AUDACITY OF DESTINY

For some unknown reason, the system did not work right, and both hardware and software departments blamed each other for the problem they had not and could not identify.

On Monday morning, during the staff meeting, the management formed a team of three engineers to evaluate the problem and nominated me to lead the team.

There we were, fake doctors, tasked with operating on a tumor based on incomplete or faulty pathology. But as we watched the test engineers conduct their tests, we gleaned they were getting wrong data at different system nodes. We also recognized we needed a data dump at those nodes.

But there was one problem: the company had only one arrogant FPGA specialist, Arthur Tucker. I'd spend hours persuading him to add a code to his firmware to provide the team with trigger points to dump data when the trigger goes off.

Right from the beginning, I had two significant problems. First, I had no access to the system software, and second, I had not studied the system data-transfer protocol. Nevertheless, we went on to review the data dump and discovered the point at which the problem started. But the cause would chew and gnaw at us for days.

In time, we went back to the data dump and reviewed the dataflow several times, shifted to the data transmission protocol, and had endless meetings. After three weeks, we came up empty.

Meanwhile, the management was in a panic mode as customers had begun to expect delivery of the system they had ordered. One day, we took copies of the data dump home. I studied it all night without a sound grasp of the protocol. As I was getting to work the following morning, Ron, stopped me at the door, then Mat arrived a few minutes later.

"I found the offending beast," Ron said.
"What did you find?" Matt asked.
"Let's say violation of data transfer protocol," Ron replied.

We met at nine o'clock with the software manager and pointed the problem out to him. Then a few minutes later, he sent Ben to join us and then we went over the bug with him. After lunch, we got together again. In the meantime, Ben had made changes to the software, so we went to the test lab and upgraded the system software after which the test team ran their test, and the system worked correctly.

The following morning, we invited management to witness the final test. When the green light came on, the senior test engineer, Steve began the demonstration. The staff watched all the nodes as the green lights went on, and the nodes printed out their data. Then Steve showed Mr. Sweeney the data he had transmitted to and printed out at each node and all the data matched.

"Steve, run the test for a few days, and let me have the result by Friday," the VP said and shook everybody's hand.

In August 1997, ADC had another major problem. BellSouth, a company located in Atlanta, GA, had bought the HFC system that did not work for them. Efforts to get the system to work failed. At the staff meeting, Mike offered me up to travel to Atlanta and evaluate the problem.

Honestly, I was angry at first, and then I thought about it and realized that he meant well—that offering me up as he did was indeed a form of flattery. I arrived at the BellSouth facility in Atlanta at nine o'clock in the morning, just as employees were coming for work. When the manager of the technical support group arrived, we met at the lobby and walked to the cafeteria for a quick breakfast. After grabbing a few bites of scrambled egg and toast, I wanted to know who was working on the system when it crashed.

"I was updating customer features when suddenly the system became unresponsive," he said. *"I powered it down and up, and it hasn't worked since then."*

Realizing the modem they used to manage the system was Courier modem—I had managed its design—I reconfigured the modem. *"OK, you can run your system,"* I said.

He entered a load command to download the system software for self-test, and the test passed. Feeling a tiny bit giddy, I gave him the telephone number to call Mr. Sweeney's office at ADC. Then we spoke

THE AUDACITY OF DESTINY

to Mr. Sweeney before I left. Immediately, when I boarded the plane and sat down, I began to write my trip report, which I finished around midnight after my return home. Then the next morning, I gave my trip report to Mr. Sweeney's secretary, Liz Ryan.

I will never forget the annual Christmas party the company hosted in 1997. I was not sure I would attend the party at first because my girlfriend, Doreen, and I had two minor children at home, and we did not have anybody to watch them. But as the night of the party drew closer, I came under pressure by Uma and Mike to attend, so I bought a fitting black suit for the occasion.

On Friday, a day before the party, Doreen's coworker, Eva, volunteered to babysit for us, so we scrambled, and found a beautiful dress for Doreen to wear. On that Saturday evening, Doreen and I arrived at the hall and joined Uma, Mike, and their wives already seated, waiting for our arrival. Then the vice president entered the room, and music began to play. Servers strolled around and served all kinds of drinks. After cocktails, the servers served different types of food. Following that, the DJ played soft music, mostly Western. When the caterers finished clearing the tables, the vice president took to the podium and delivered his annual remark.

Then Uma took over; *"I am proud to announce that this year's Key Contributor Award goes to my department and a deserving engineer of African descent, Chuks I. Ndukwe."*

I got up, surprised to receive the award. And for that reason, I did not know what to say except to thank the VP, Uma and Mike, and the employees for the honor they gave me so unexpectedly.

As it's always the case, although not easily discernible, our innerguide lets us know when our time is up on any given endeavor. So one day, when I was finishing a report on the project I'd just completed, a call came from a gentleman, Jim Reeves, the president of Common

Chuks I. Ndukwe

Agenda. We spoke for one hour and a half during which he wanted to set me up for an interview with Lucent Technologies. *"What's their main product?"* I asked. *"Lucent is among the leading manufacturers of the Internet gateway, and VOIP,"* he said.

Then he set up an interview for me with Lucent Technologies in New Providence, New Jersey, which I attended and got the job.

Chapter 13

THE AUDACITY OF DESTINY

The Grand Finale

An ending was an ending. No matter how many pages of sentences and paragraphs of great stories led up to it, it would always have the last word.

~ Sarah Dessen

Chuks I. Ndukwe

Laudable

I don't expect congratulations for successful beginning, what I want is the applause at successful ending.

~ Amit Kalantri

The first time I set foot inside Lucent Technologies' world headquarters, which used to be AT&T, it was for an interview. The hiring manager, John Tsimaras, walked up to me in the lobby, introduced himself, and led the way up the stairs and along a winding hallway to the PathStar department. Then he showed me around before we walked back along the same corridor to the cafeteria for tea and coffee and walked back—good morning exercise! Then John began the interview. After the meeting, I got the usual questions: "How much are you looking for?" And as always, I declined to negotiate.

I returned to Minnesota and got a call from Mr. Sarath. We chatted for a while between hold-on and I-am-backs and reached an acceptable offer. Then I gave my two weeks' notice to ADC and joined Lucent in summer 1998. Before leaving Minnesota, Lucent arranged for my relocation and a temporary residence in New Jersey—Best Western hotel across the street from the office at 1600 Mountain Avenue, Murray Hill.

Reporting for work on Monday, I attended a weekly meeting presided over by the chief technical officer, Mr. Phil Winters. He had familiarity with every project the department was working on and also directed the Bell Labs' software research department. Two weeks later, John gave me an assignment: to design a timing-distribution board for

THE AUDACITY OF DESTINY

the PathStar system. So I began by developing specifications for the board—the only way I had started every projects.

I completed the document in time and catalogued the parts I intended to use in the design and their functional characteristics. Phil presided over the meeting spent discussing the paper; 'Timing Distribution Design Specifications.' At the end of the session, he complimented me for a fantastic job on the material. *"The job is half-done. Hand it over to John Parks,"* he said. *"I've some engineers in the demo room who do not know what they are doing down there. I want you to go there and get that system working."*

I'd go home that evening and chew on how to join the team, without seeming to be a condescending smartass. Then at the cafeteria the following morning, I joined the group—Prasad, Nikhil, Yan, and Andrew with my oatmeal and toast.

"Do you think we can get the system working today?" I inquired.

They ignored me and continued to eat and share jokes. Trifling arrogant sons of bi***es—they seemed. It became apparent that they did not want me around, so I had to get to the system before them. When they arrived, I was entering a command on the keyboard with a telephone handset on my ear and not getting any sound as specified in the test procedure. So I took the document with me, made a copy for myself, came back to the demo room, and gave the material back to Prasad. *"Stand aside and watch us,"* he said. Then I reported the matter to Phil.

"I expect you to elbow your way in and take over the damn project not to be their pal," Phil said.

I was left wondering how nasty I should be to get the job done. But to bring an impactful attitude and perspective on the matter, I had to understand the problem much better. So I took the test procedure to my office and studied it. Then I went back to Phil and demanded changes to the test procedure.

"Why?" he asked.

"The test should start with verification of the data path," I said. *"This test procedure does not specify that."*

"See Ken Thompson," he said, and my eyes popped wide open.

Lest you wonder why, Ken's an icon, the author of the C programming language textbook I'd used in college. I confess cowardice to not knowing how to approach him. I was very intimidated. So after dragging my feet, I went to see Ken and told him what I had in mind.

"That's a brilliant idea," he said. "How much of software coding do you know?" I pinched myself after hearing Ken describe my idea as brilliant.

"Quite a bit. We used your book on C programming language in class," I said quietly.

"Well then, I'll give you the DSP coefficients for the signals, and you can do it yourself," he said.

"I couldn't; I am not on the Babine server. I am currently doing hardware," I replied.

"OK, come back after lunch," he said.

After obtaining Ken's approval, I informed the engineers of my intention to modify the test procedure, which drew forth predictable looks of contempt upon their faces.

"Aren't you the new hardware engineer?" Prasad asked. "How do you know what we are doing?"

"I'm asking myself the same question," I said.

Now provoked by Prasad's peevish, provocative meanness which seemed like a look-down-upon attitude, I went to Ken's office, came back with a new chip, and took the whole chassis apart.

> **I figured out that the best way to fight disrespect and insult on the job is to thrive where others have failed.**

So I waited for the group to come back to the demo room so they could watch me replace the chip and put the chassis together. When they came back, I began to put the interface block together and watched them lose themselves in disbelief, not saying anything but just watching, obviously struck by disbelief syndrome my actions inflicted

THE AUDACITY OF DESTINY

on them. But that's not an accident, that's how I wanted them to feel.

There are times when, because I am black, I let insults slide. But that time, I wanted to make a statement, not with words but with actions.

So I pushed the router back into its slot, powered the system up, and went from the first slot to the last, issuing commands and listening for the prescribed tones. By the time I finished the exercise, I had found that three slots were not producing any sound.

"We are almost there," I told the group with a convincing voice that reflected my inner feeling.

Then I went back to Ken and told him what I had found.

"That's fantastic. Come back in thirty minutes for a new chip," he said. Now I am thinking, *"I might make it,"* after hearing Ken describe my finding as fantastic.

After messing around for one hour, I went back to Ken's office and returned to the demo room with a revised chip. Then I tested the new chip, and all the time slots gave out tones as required.

"The system is working now," I told the group and reported to Phil.

"I want you to show me how it is working," he demanded.

Like a proud soldier who's just accomplished his mission, I marched to the demo room followed by Phil, and I repeated the test.

"That's brilliant. I knew you could rise to the occasion," he said.

Hyperbole apart, I felt I've found my footing—a coveted spot among the elite team of communication engineers. On Monday, after the weekly meeting presided over by Phil, he told me to get ready to travel to Naperville, Illinois, to help debug a new system that division had designed for us.

"Can you leave tonight?" The director, Al, asked.

"I can leave right now if necessary," I answered.

"OK, let me make a call," he said.

He called Connie, Lucent's travel manager and made arrangements for my travel to Chicago that evening. Connie made reservations at Days Inn, 1350 East Ogden Avenue in Naperville and car with Avis

Chuks I. Ndukwe

Rent a Car. So I arrived at O'Hare airport, picked up the car at Avis's office, drove to Naperville, and checked in at Days Inn.

On Monday, I reported to Lucent's facility at 2000 Naperville Road and met the manager of the hardware development department, Mr. Hinterlong and his engineers, Dave and Vince. After spending four weeks with them debugging the system, we had some drinks at the hotel before Mr. Hinterlong, Dave, and Vince went home. Then I spent the night writing my trip report. And I returned to New Jersey on Saturday.

One week later, Phil gave me a new assignment to design a new Voice Over IP system. I began to write my product design specifications immediately. Once I had finished it, I called a meeting to review the original design concept. Then I completed the product design and the schedule and had both discussed in a meeting presided over by Phil himself.

"This is how every project should look like," he said. *"I think you are on a roll."*

At the next Monday meeting, Phil announced that John had quit and a new manager, Dr. Chris Autry, would be taking over. A week later, Chris arrived and took over the management of the department. Chris had just received his doctorate in electrical engineering from the University of North Carolina. On Friday, I had continued to work on my board—in the lab way past the closing time. Then Chris walked into the lab just as I was about to lock the door.

"How is it going, Chuks?" he asked.

"It is going pretty well. Just finished debugging the second board this week," I said.

So to prove it, I placed a call through my board to him. We talked on the phone; then we hung up and went home. I completed the project and released it to the system-testing department one month ahead of schedule. Two weeks later, Chris crashed into my office and shook my hand. *"Release Comdac, (my project) to the factory for production,"* he said, *"It passed the final test flawlessly."* I recognized right away that I had made a good impression upon Chris.

Meanwhile, start-up companies were springing up all over the

THE AUDACITY OF DESTINY

United States. Engineers were leaving their companies to join start-ups. On the flip side, the Internet was crashing and taking a long time to recover. Cisco Systems was beating the daylights out of Lucent Technologies because Lucent's PathStar system router was subpar and customers were returning it.

One day Chris invited me to his office for a short meeting to discuss his trip to North Carolina and said, *"I've appointed you as my delegate, so you will attend the staff meeting and represent the department on Monday."*

So we went over the statuses of all the active projects. Then on Monday morning, I attended the meeting at the vice president's conference room—scared and intimidated. But in the end, I did a pretty good job representing Chris. So from that day, Chris and I met every Friday after work and discussed project issues and courses of action. I recalled one Monday morning in June 1999, and rumor had it, Phil had come up with a solution for Internet rampant crashes he called high-availability feature (HA). It turned out all Internet-gateway-equipment manufacturers bought computers from Intel to manage their systems, and they were equally affected by the occasional crashes. The HA feature involves two systems—primary, and a secondary, interchanging logical system control when one goes down to avoid Internet downtime.

One day, Chris invited me to accompany him to Al's office for a long meeting he spent persuading Al to promote me to the manager of the PathStar department instead of hiring somebody new. *"Give me a few days to chew on it,"* Al said. A few weeks later, an e-mail came out announcing Chris Autry's resignation and my promotion to a manager of the department. Phil had also left Lucent to start a new company in California. Shortly, four engineers resigned and joined Chris at his new start-up, Tellium Inc.

So, upon taking over the department, I had lost four experienced engineers and inherited two persistent problems, one of which had existed for two years. The pressure to resolve these issues was profound—to put it mildly. I had once bragged that I was a strategist. So I had to demonstrate that now.

With that in mind, I hired two experienced engineers, Lee Glinski and John Lu. Both gifted but not adept in the field of telecommunication engineering. I let them chose their projects among the old and the new routers. And I became their mentor at that crucial moment. So we began to delve into the heart of the real issues.

We had one PathStar system in the lab. So John and I hooked up oscilloscopes at critical points and set up triggers on the power-control circuitry. It ran for one day and crashed. After a thorough review of the signal-events before and after the trigger, we found that the two Intel computers that controlled the HA feature were in contention with each other, causing the systems to crash.

With the print out of the images of the signals before and after the crash, I invited the Intel and Lucent managers to a meeting to discuss the result of our experiment. When the meeting began, William described the feature and the control mechanism and provided us with the Boolean equation they had implemented. Immediately when he handed the Boolean table to me, I noticed the problem and drew his attention to a specific point in the state machine when two power supplies came on at the same time, either by a glitch or on purpose.

"That is the problem," I said. *"You designed contention into the product."*

"If that is the cause, we can prove it right away," John Parkes said.

"How do you intend to do that?" I asked.

"We can delay the voltage rise time of one power supply and see how the computers will assign control," he said.

So we followed John to the lab, and there he turned both systems on simultaneously, and the systems crashed. Then he made the changes he had recommended and turned both systems on simultaneously again, and the systems did not crash this time. He tried several times, and the systems remained stable.

In the end, we agreed that Intel would fix the Boolean equation as a

THE AUDACITY OF DESTINY

long-term solution while we continued with our temporary fixes. To prove the fix, John gave the modified system to the test department to initiate a disruptive test to crash the system. At the next staff meeting, the test department manager reported that his systems had stopped stalling after Chuks and his engineer made some changes on the chassis.

"*Test it for two more weeks,*" the VP said. "*If it continues to hold, do the fixes on all the systems. Chuks, I might want to borrow your engineers to go to the field and make the changes.*"

"That won't be a problem, sir," I said.

However, we still had to focus on the router problem. So at the next staff meeting, I announced the beginning of the new 120 MHz router project in parallel with the debugging of the ailing 66 MHz routers.

While John Lu and Lee Glinski were working on the hardware, I began to dissect the firmware to figure out its structure. I finished reviewing the source code and decided to redesign the whole program, and announced my intention in the next meeting, assuring the staff we would not impact the current project. I'd decided to change the design to a hierarchical modular structure, and sought approval from the software director, Mr. Scordo. Surprisingly, he welcomed the new design ideas and urged me to go ahead with it.

While I was reviewing the signal and variable names, I stumbled over one specific signal name which was described as a buffer but routed outside the block and back inside, in complete violation of VHDL rules. Therefore, I redefined it as in/out and proceeded with my work. I finished the global-signal definition, segregated the code into modules, and compiled it with a few syntax errors. After correcting the mistakes, I burned the EPROM and gave copies to John and Lee to run the two routers in the PathStar system overnight, and both routers worked without glitches. So I released John's board to the test department while Lee and I continued to work on his board—to get it to run at 120 MHz, but the closest we got was 100 MHz then two weeks later, I announced the successful completion of both routers.

At the next staff meeting, the test department manager, Pat announced that both the 66 MHz and 100 MHz routers had passed the test, so we released both routers to the factory for production.

It was a memorable time for me. Because before the meeting adjourned, Mr. Scordo stood up and reminded the staff how long they had worked on both the router and the internet problems and urged the executive team to give my department and me a standing ovation. As if in a dream, rumor had begun to spread that Lucent's stock had taken a hit on Wall Street because the company had recorded its quarterly earnings incorrectly. A few days later, the president of Lucent conducted a companywide teleconference and gave official confirmation of the rumor.

> **The day I was laid off was the point, at which my rise in the technological world started to stall, and the unwinding began—it was a slow and painful walk home.**

A few weeks later, Lucent laid off over forty thousand employees and closed several divisions. However, Lee, John, and I were transferred to Bell labs—probably to reward our performances. But nine months later, September 2001, we got laid off. I panicked and bought a franchise that turned out to be a scam. And so my life began to unravel.

> **However, I've to say that to the extent I've done anything right or achieved any success in this industry, the credit solely belongs to Northeastern University's visionary educational system—"the co-op." The co-op opens the window for students to take a glimpse into those few easily-overlooked aspects of engineering even before the graduating students take their yearbook pictures and receive their commencements notices.**

Chapter 14

THE AUDACITY OF DESTINY

Marriage and Family

All happy families are alike; each unhappy family is unhappy in its own way.

~ Leo Tolstoy, Anna Karenina

Chuks I. Ndukwe

Shattered Lives and Faith

What is stronger than the human heart which shatters over and over and still lives.

~ Rupi Kaur

Growing up in a culture in which two families arranged marriages for their children and dating was a strange notion, discouraged, and in most cases unacceptable as per the norms of social mores, I felt like I was standing at the gates of hell. I knew the kind of girl my family would choose for me would certainly not be the kind I'd sit next to—even in the church. I am naturally attracted to the type of girls other men find sassy, brash, or intimidating—go figure!

There's one girl like that in my town by the name Mgborie Onwuegbu, but she was entirely out of my league being the daughter of a wealthy, influential businessman and a girl who grew up in the township of Calabar of all places. So we did not cross paths until the period I was spending my first holidays at Aba from the technical college. I was on scholarship by then by Star Brewery Aba, and the company had rented a room for me—across the street from my uncle's house. Disappointingly, you could see my door from my uncle's.

One Sunday afternoon, Mgborie knocked on my door, and I opened the door and let her in. She was dressed to provoke some raw emotions. On the first visit of hers, we spent quite some time talking about school and the fun of spending holidays at Aba. *"Your uncle Utali is very proud of you,"* she said, *"he can't stop boasting about your admission to the technical college on Brewery's scholarship."* The more we interacted, the more a discernable dynamics began to develop between us, so I began to foresee the possibility of avoiding the hell I dreaded.

THE AUDACITY OF DESTINY

Suddenly, I remembered that her father is locked in a land dispute with my uncles. As is often the case, land dispute leads to loss of lives sometimes. So there we were, cheerful, happy, imagining close relationship, and having so much fun together but this crushing thought of land dispute intruded on our fantasies and got in the way. *"Get dressed,"* she said, *"let's go to the Sunday jump—dance party for students on holidays."* We went to the jump and had a fantastic time dancing and joking.

Mgborie visited the following Sunday, and as we were leaving for the jump, my uncle's wife saw us together. Then later in the evening, she cautioned me to be careful because our family members would not approve of my sneaking around with Mgborie. So I began to avoid her, and what could have been a new friendship or possible marriage died a slow and painful death.

The day I first met the next girl I liked who'd become my wife, I was working at the Nigerian petroleum refinery in Eleme, Nigeria. I had graduated from technical college a few months before, and because I was much younger than the men I supervised, I'd ran errands for them while they did anything that I asked them to do without pressuring them to do it. Respect for older people is one of Ibo dominant cultural values, and people claim certain unalienable birthrights based on age.

One day, I'd gone to a small store across the street from the refinery to buy cookies for the men I supervised. It was there that I met a girl in the store. We clashed over the novel *Young Love* (authored by a nineteen-year-old girl) she was reading. I had read it before and knew it was about a boyfriend, virginity, sex, cheating, and betrayal. She was a high school student on Christmas holiday and seemed to be the no-nonsense type I am attracted to, so I invited her to visit me before going back to school. Talking on the phone was not an option because the phone did not exist anywhere except at the post offices.

At the age of twelve, I had developed a deep sense of respect and

Chuks I. Ndukwe

appreciation for girls; I even thought of them as angels when they rallied around my mom and performed their angelic wonders by transforming my mom from near-death to a spiritual marvel. I'd always felt that it was their young, loving, and caring hearts that had brought Mom back from the brink of death—when she was grieving the death of her only daughter.

It was with that mindset that I started dating her—my first steady girlfriend. She loved Mom and marveled at her spirituality. Mom adored her, and her mother liked me equally. Then the war began and compelled us to live together—at different places that I was sent to build an electrical plant for the refinery until the end of the war.

Four days before I departed Nigeria for the United States, she insisted on getting married before my departure, and I worried about the unknown—the future and the inevitable challenges that would come later if things go wrong. Still, I had no reason to say no, so I consented, and we got married. Then four days later, on December 9, 1972, I boarded the plane and was on my way to the United States.

One Saturday in 1977, five years after I'd departed Nigeria, my wife joined me in Boston, Massachusetts. From what I observed, she looked different—overcast by much less attractive demeanor than her usual self. On June 1, 1998, our first daughter, Ere, arrived prematurely when her mother's water broke.

In many ways, the birth of our daughter Ere gave our marriage a jump start. When I took Fortune to the hospital, women in labor were screaming so loud I almost cried and went home after the nurse wheeled her to the delivery room; I was unable to stay in the waiting room.

After the birth of our daughter, Fortune went back to school full time early in September. She gave the baby a bath in the evening, went to bed, woke up at ten, and went to work from eleven at night to seven in the morning. I kept the baby at night, gave her a bath in the morning, took her to the babysitter, picked her up after classes, and took her

THE AUDACITY OF DESTINY

home, and her mother took over till she went to sleep at six in the evening. As you can see, I handled it well. And that thing about a baby keeping the mother awake all night, Yes! I know a little bit about that too. One day, I discovered that my wife had had a baby before joining me and each time I asked her about it, she'd refuse to talk about it and snap at me and said, "I will not talk about it until the time comes."

I suspect you expect me to have shouted, cursed, thrown my fist, or broken something. No, I did not do any of that; instead, I collected my thoughts. I began to plan immediately in my mind to send Fortune to Nigeria to bring the baby to the United States to be with his mother, only if she would say, "Yes, I had a baby in Nigeria before coming over." She could have added, "It's not your business," and it would not have mattered.

On April 20, 1980, my second daughter, Ugo, arrived full term, a fat, plump baby. I continued to beg Fortune to talk to me about her son, but she refused. *"When the time comes,"* she said every single time.

On September 4, 1985, my third, last, and the youngest daughter, Chika, arrived. We moved to a three-family rental property we bought in Brockton, Massachusetts. I'd kneel and beg Fortune to talk about the baby at midnight, midday, six o'clock in the morning, and the evening. And Fortune continued to insist that she would talk about the baby only when the time came. So I began to wonder what time she had in mind, and when the time will come. If she could say "when the time comes". Why couldn't she utter one word—'yes'?

I had attended the Fourth of July celebration at the American consulate when I was in high school, and I had fallen in love with America the first time I read the preamble to the American Declaration of Independence:

"We hold these truths to be self-evident, that all men are created equal, that they are endowed, by their Creator, with certain unalienable Rights, that among these are Life, Liberty, and the pursuit of

Chuks I. Ndukwe

Happiness."
    I'd cherished those words, liberty in particular; the word 'Liberty' is like life itself to me ever since I had heard it. So eager to make a decision based on that word 'Liberty' I tried one more time. *"Please, Fortune, please talk to me about that baby. Please say yes," I insisted.*
    "I said when the time comes," she said yet again.
    "I hate to say these words: that time will never come for me," I said, although not wanting to give up. *"Consider this marriage over, because you have denied me the liberty to exercise rare goodwill most men would find difficult to extend to their wives in a situation like this."*
    Soon after, I moved my personal belongings to the guest room without yelling or cursing. And without letting the children know what had happened. In a way, I was happy that we'd had three children at that moment because we had planned to have three children if we were fertile—when Fortune and I were dating, in love, and planning the future. It all seemed like the distant past now, shrouded in the mists of time.
    For the most part, though, taking care of the children, watching them crash in and out of the door with their friends to drink some juice and run out again, made my life after work so worthwhile.
    Running bathwater, giving them baths, and sitting around after dinner to talk about school and set goals gave me a sense of assurance that they would be OK.
    Dropping them off at school, watching them wave back, and run back to class made me feel as if they were on the right track to appreciating school and wanting to learn.
    And teaching them how to deal with bullies at school, rules at home, and deciding together after dinner what kind of punishment to give for minor infractions, made us seem like a typical, functional family. So we were still happy, even the troublemakers who got spanked with a soft flat paper paddle or with my finger.
    One day in 1990, on a blistering summer day, when I was on my way home from work, Chika ran out to greet me as I was parking my car.

THE AUDACITY OF DESTINY

"Daddy," she called out to me, almost sobbing. *"You won't believe what happened today."*

"What happened, sweetheart?" I asked.

"People in long white robes with long beards came to our house," she said. *"They lit candles and incense everywhere; they sang and danced; they sprinkled water and powder everywhere in our house, and they said that they were driving an evil spirit away. Daddy, do you know who the evil spirit is?"*

"No, sweetheart, what did they say?" I asked her instead.

"Daddy, they said that you are the evil spirit," she said and broke out in tears.

"So, what do you think?" I asked her again, urging her to say everything that was on her mind.

"You are not the evil spirit," she said, crying. *"You are the best daddy in the whole world."*

"Stop crying," I said to her. *"The most important thing is what you think. Come on, let's have some ice cream."*

While we were still eating ice cream, Fortune walked in and told the kids about a revival they were having at church. So I learned for the first time that she was involved with the cult called Cherubim and Seraphim—founded in Nigeria.

On Sunday, the day of the revival, I went to church with them—my children and their mother, to ease the worries in Chika's mind about her father being an evil spirit. When the revival started, the priest announced my name as one of the very special invitees; there were seven of us, to be exact.

The pulpit was transformed into a decorated shaded altar as dark-bluish smoke rose out of it and filled the church. The atmosphere was beautiful and serene. People came out in front of the congregation and confessed their transgressions, and the high priest admonished the transgressors.

The highlight came as the high priest came out in an elaborate, amazingly decorated red-and-white robe, surrounded by the priests and the prophets. Buried in the dark smoke that poured out of the altar, the congregation rose, and loud music began to play as he stood at the center of the church and announced the names of the people who he said should change their evil ways. I wasn't sure whether those people he called out were even in the church.

The finale arrived when the music began to play again. The special invitees lined up behind the prophets as the prophetesses trailed, and we danced around and around the church. Then the high priest said the closing prayer. I turned and looked at my children while we were dancing around the isles and Chika seemed petrified, from the look on her face. Then the congregation rose and joined in the dance, and the occasion came to a choreographed end.

Before we left the church, one of the priests escorted my family and me to the parking lot.

"We are glad you could come today," he said. *"I look forward to seeing you every Sunday."*

"I came to hear you call me an evil spirit as you did in my house—in my absence and front of my children," I said.

"Oh, I thought you came to worship with us," he said and left.

"Yeah, why didn't the big priest tell Daddy that he's an evil spirit?" Chika asked.

"His spirit is too strong," their mother said.

"Daddy, I was scared when you were dancing behind the big priest," Chika said.

"Are you happy now?" I asked her.

"Yes, Daddy. I hate those priests," she said.

"Chika! Don't say that," Ugo warned her.

I had bought my second house at 27 Pleasant Street, Brockton, Massachusetts, the next street down from our first house. Shortly, Fortune moved to a two-bedroom apartment. So I rented all six apartments in the two properties out to tenants with Section 8 government housing assistance.

In an earlier chapter, I recalled the trip I made to Nigeria to have my immigrant visa processed. During that trip, I filed for expedited divorce due to time constraint and the fact that I had a civil marriage in

THE AUDACITY OF DESTINY

Nigeria. The judge granted me a divorce, but I did not give Fortune her copy of the divorce decree when I came back, hoping things could change for the better.

After I had been offered a job in Chicago and told my children, Fortune said the kids that they were not going anywhere with me. So I rented out the two properties we owned with gross rental income of three thousand, two hundred and twenty-five dollars per month. At this moment, it had become apparent that the model family I had hoped to build was not going to happen. So I went to the Housing and Urban Development (HUD) office with her and put my renters on direct deposit because their rents were coming from the government. Before I left for Chicago, I gave Fortune copies of the deeds for the two houses, our real estate–account checkbook, and my personal-account checkbook, which I had made joint. Then I introduced her to my attorney in case she needed legal help. Finally, I gave her my divorce decree and left after hugging my children.

I believed by doing all these things, I had set her up pretty well for life, and she would not have any problem taking care of the needs of our children. But for me, it was a clean break.

Shortly after I arrived in Chicago, I began to get calls from my friends in Boston that Fortune was telling them that she did not move to Chicago with me because I was trying to kill her.

In 1993, three years after I had left Brockton, Fortune left our minor children alone and traveled to Nigeria. Once when I made my nightly call to my children, Chika told me, *"Daddy, Mommy left us alone and went to Nigeria. Please, Daddy, don't tell anybody."* It was an awkward moment for me because her action was child neglect and child endangerment—serious enough for me to pursue custody. But I would never dream of separating my children from their mother.

I recalled the events that took place when my children visited me in Minnesota with their mother. Well, after that visit, she left Brockton and moved to Florida to live and hid my children from me for three years. Watching Fortune act in this way—against the best interest of her children, I felt compelled to tolerate but still questioned her motherly instincts. So I agonized for years believing that God would lead me to my children.

One weekend, I had gone to Boston without anybody in mind: it was such a spontaneous action without forethought. I had to believe that the trip was forced on me by a higher power for a purpose beyond my understanding. When I arrived in Boston, I decided to visit an old friend, Dr. Everett Onuoha. I arrived at his house, but the door was locked, and nobody answered the doorbell. As I turned around to leave, his wife, Ester, was getting out of her car in the parking lot.

"Mr. Ndukwe, stop," a voice yelled. I stopped and turned around, and Ester was running toward me. *"I am just coming back from Florida,"* she said. *"I spent some time with your kids. Come inside; let me call them. I want you to talk to those kids."*

So she called them up.

"Hello, Ugo, hold on," she said and gave me the phone.

"Ugo, this is Daddy. How are you?" I asked.

Ugo kept quiet for a while; then she hung the phone up.

"Don't worry. I have Fortune's number and address. What Fortune is doing to those kids is shameful," Ester said.

I was overwhelmed because I had predicted that God would lead me to where my kids were without my going anywhere to search for them. But I never knew it would happen this way.

"Thank you so much, Ester," I said, grateful for her help.

"You are welcome," she said. *"I am sorry I can't offer you anything because I am just returning from my vacation."*

"Where is Dr. Onuoha?" I asked.

Ester paused before she began sharing her marital problems with me.

"Oh dear, I am so sorry," I said sympathetically.

"It's OK. Here is Dr. Onuoha's address. The kids are there," she said. *"Go and see him. The kids would love to see their favorite uncle,*

THE AUDACITY OF DESTINY

Chuks."

Now high from the information about my children, I stopped briefly at Dr. Onuoha's and got mobbed by his children.

"Chuks, my man, I didn't think that I'd ever see you again," he said.

"OK professor, you thought wrong," I said. *"Out of sight does not always translate to out of mind."*

We chatted for a while; then, I returned to New Jersey. A week later, I called my kids in Florida, and Chika picked up the phone.

"Hello," she answered.

"Chika, how are you?" I greeted her.

She kept quiet for a while and hung the phone up. It was a slow start to our eventual reunion. Now four weeks had passed since I made contact with my children and I've had time to think about the immense pain they might be feeling and the suffering that they had endured for all that time.

Now memory takes me back to my childhood, and I remembered how lost, empty, and hopeless I felt when either of my parents stayed out later than my brother and I expected. I thought about the intensity of my feelings and how nobody and nothing could calm me down except the sight of my parents and my mother's sweet voice. I remembered accusing my parents of not thinking about me and my brother and how it did not matter whether or not they had good reasons for staying out late; I simply warned them not to stay out late again. So now, I am reminded painfully how my children feel due to the actions of both of their parents. So I decided to go to Florida and see them.

On Labor Day 1999, I traveled to Maryland with my girlfriend, Renee. We arrived at my cousin Onwuchekwa's house early in the evening. After dinner, I told him I would be going to Florida alone, and my girlfriend would stay with them while I was gone.

"No, Uncle, I will not let you drive to Florida alone," he said. *"It's too far. I'll go with you and share the driving."*

So we left Maryland very early in the morning to beat the traffic and reached Tampa late at night.

The following day, my children visited me at the hotel I was staying.

"I am sorry that Mom and Dad put you through such a shameful ordeal," I told my kids. "I wish things were different. You can count on my abiding and unconditional love."

"Mommy told me that you did not want me when I was born. Why?" Chika asked.

"Do you believe her?" I asked her. "How can you forget how happy I used to be playing with you?"

"Why didn't you come and look for us?" Ugo asked.

"I did not know where you were," I said.

"Why did you abandon us?" Ere asked.

"First of all, your mother had a son with another man," I said. "And then when I asked her about it, she insulted me by refusing to talk to me about the baby for five years. Second, she refused to move to Chicago with me. No! I did not abandon you."

"Yes, her son is here now, and she says that he is our brother. No, he is not our brother! It is all her fault. I hate her," Ere said, her voice dripping with all the bottled-up anger.

"Yes, it's her fault," Chika and Ugo agreed.

I intervened instinctively to defend their mother.

"Please stop. I am here to reunite with you not to chastise your mother. So can we promise not to separate again?" I asked.

"Look at what she's done," Ugo said.

"Let's stop blaming your mother," I urged out of some sense of fairness, "She's not a bad woman. Everybody makes mistakes."

Later that evening, I took them out to their favorite restaurant. Ugo was working for Time Warner and attending college, and her job was paying her tuition fees. Ere was in the military, so I chatted with Chika about the college to which she intended to seek admission.

"Ugo, what do you want from Daddy?" I asked her.

"Daddy, I want a Honda," she said.

"OK, can you direct me to the dealership?" I asked.

When we got to the Honda dealership, I bought a Honda Accord

THE AUDACITY OF DESTINY

for her. The next day, Onwuchekwa and I returned to Maryland then Renee, and I returned to New Jersey the following day.

After the trip, I could not contain myself because now I could talk to my children and despite my poor vocal ability, I sang the song, "Amazing Grace" or "My God how wonderful thou art" every time I was in the shower which was my favorite place for singing. You guessed it—the running water hides my weak singing voice.

So this reunification with my children conjured the past up for me—their childhood when we used to be happy with each other. It also restored our father-daughter dynamics. I'd get a phone call from one of my daughters to tell me she's on her way home from school or work.

On the late hours of Saturday nights, I'd get a call from either one, two, or all of them to inform me that they were on their way home from the club as some boys' voices lingered at the background. Then I'd inquire as to who the boys were. And I would get *"Dadeeeh, nobody"* in answer. What gave me the most comfort was that when I tried to caution them, I'd get, *"Yeah daddy we know, there's a time for everything"* —which was the lesson I had taught them in the early years of their lives.

One day, in 2000, as I was surfing the web for what I can't remember now, I came across a posting about Nigerian youth convention to be held in New Jersey. I recalled attending such events in high school and how thrilled I'd felt meeting people and making friends. So I sent plane tickets to Ugo and Chika. The day they arrived in Newark airport, I waited at the baggage claim area, as they made their way out. Immediately when they saw me, they jumped on me, and all of us fell to the ground—built up emotion that time has provided its release valve.

That spontaneous outburst of emotion and public expression of affection has stayed fresh in my mind since that visit; it was a demonstration of love between a father and his children, and their enduring relationship. It was merely a practical expression of our family dynamics. I have to say; my children's visit seemed like a portrayal of the healing of shattered young lives although the scars remained visible.

Chuks I. Ndukwe

If you'd ask me to describe myself as a father, I'd tell you that I am a guardian, caretaker, a teacher, a friend, and a disciplinarian who ought to be close to his children to do his job right.

Meanwhile, the process of normalizing my family relationship occurred in 2008 when Chika came with her sisters, and her mother to seek my approval to marry Dr. Nnanna's son, her boyfriend. At this moment, my financial life was barely hanging by a thread, as I could not afford a bus ticket to anywhere outside Newark where I lived. But my niece Grace, and her husband Tunde, my nephew Chima and his wife Nenna stepped in and hosted the reception. Honest, they were all I had at the time.

For the most part, my marriage did one crucial thing for me—it affirmed for me the integrity of the concept of the human interiority complex. [the awesome Irresistible inner-power, conscience, non-carnal senses, and the inner-voice] And how these four work in contingent symbiosis to move life along the guard-rails of the natural order.

I had stated that the non-carnal senses can look beyond the bright light of day and the darkness of night to see the future and what is yet to occur although obscured in currency. Earlier in my childhood, I had expressed my fears that I might not have children of my own or that something would go wrong between my children and me. I had these feelings because of how children would use the power of their irresistible and adorable faces that impel pity to force me to play with them until they fell asleep and I'd complain to Mom and opined about it.

Thinking about it now, it seems as though my non-carnal senses saw all these coming. And God fed me with enough of children's love—in those bygone days.

The fantastic thing about all these is that I have had several relationships with ladies who had children since my divorce and each of them was thrilled with my loving attitude towards their children—just one of the few reasons they fell in love with me.

Although the pain of losing the most precious gift God ever gave me—my children will never decrease; however, I sometimes feel

THE AUDACITY OF DESTINY

vindicated because I have all these women surrounding me with their children as though to ease the pain in my heart.

During this moment of my life, I experienced a different type of pain—what my children would think of me and how they would feel about me marrying another woman. I say this because I had not revealed my divorce from their mother to them—not yet. But when I finally told them and was ready to propose to my fiancée, cancer snatched her from me—she died.

Chapter 15

THE AUDACITY OF DESTINY

Helping Hands Abound

There is no exercise better for the heart than reaching down and lifting people up.

~ John Holmes

THE AUDACITY OF DESTINY

Good Deeds

A good deed is never lost; he who sows courtesy reaps friendship, and he who plants kindness gathers love.

~ St. Basil

Each time I take a peek through the keyhole of life into memory's veiled spaces, I see dogs chasing me around several blocks of College Road in Burlington, Massachusetts. Then I recall my first experience of American generosity. I had just arrived in the US—six months before. One afternoon, when I was returning from work, dogs began to bark and chase after me then an old lady who lived across the street from Terry Zdanauk—the lady I was living with, called out to me.

"*Son, come here,*" she said.

I went over to her, thinking she wanted me to do something for her.

"*Yes, ma'am,*" I said.

"*I see the dogs chasing and barking at you every time you come out of Terry's house, and I feel terrible for you. Do you know how to drive?*"

"No, ma'am, I do not," I said, without knowing where she was going with this line of conversation.

"*Go and learn how to drive,*" she said. "*I have a car for you so those stupid dogs will stop chasing after you.*"

Then I came home and told Terry what Miss Wendy told me. So she ran over across the street to Miss Wendy's and came back with a new Toyota Corolla and the title. "*Go and thank Miss Wendy,*" Terry said. So I ran over to Miss Wendy's house and thanked her for the car.

Chuks I. Ndukwe

At that point, Terry parked the car in her driveway and made an appointment for my driving lessons. After four lessons, I got my driver's license and became the proud owner of a brand new standard shift Toyota Corolla.

My second experience was in 1985. I had escorted Larry, a coworker at Codex Corporation, to inspect a house he wanted to buy in Brockton, Massachusetts. The realtor was not in the office when we arrived, so we sat in his lobby to wait for him. Lacking a good topic for discussion and naturally not fluid at it, I threw the problems I was having with my telephone interface project at Larry seeking suggestions I knew he was not capable of offering. Then I saw a man limping rather severely, trying to crawl up the steps. So I dashed out of the office and helped him get up the steps. He was not a small man, by any measure:

> **I remember his right hand around my neck as I held it with my right hand, and my left hand around his waist. Then we walked up the steps one at a time until we got to the top. And I surrendered my seat to him.**

"Sir, the realtor, is not in the office," I said. *"Have a seat. We are all waiting for him."*

"I'm the realtor," he replied.

Anyway, I opened the office door, and he went inside his office. Soon he came out and gave a couple who had sat beside Larry a check, and then they walked out without saying thank-you. Then he talked to another couple before taking Larry and me to the house Larry had come to inspect.

"What do you think?" he asked Larry.

"Beautiful," Larry answered. *"But I have to bring my wife to see it before we continue."*

"I will hold it for you if you put something down on it," the realtor

THE AUDACITY OF DESTINY

said. Finally, Larry said, *"I'll come back. I don't have any money or my checkbook with me."*

Before we left the realtor's office, he gave me his business card while Larry was in the restroom, and asked me to come back alone and see him. He wrote, *"Helped up the steps"* on the back of the card. So I went back the next day during my lunch break and knocked on his door.

"Come in, young man," he said. *"Can I help you?"*

I gave him the business card he had given me the previous day.

"Oh yes, have a seat," he said, recalling who I was in that instant.

The realtor, whose name was Mr. Schumer, as I had gleaned from the card he had given me, gave me a short sermon on good deeds, empathy, and humanity—and the reward of treating others as one would like others to treat oneself. Honestly, I had no idea that what I had done counted as a good deed, so I was taken aback.

"Do you own a house, or just renting an apartment?" he asked.

"I'm renting an apartment," I answered.

He told me about his first house on Wilmington Street. *"I've made lots of money off that house since then,"* he said. Then he talked about the couple he had given a check the previous day.

"That couple was my daughter and her boyfriend," he said. *"They come here; they sit around the house, and they watch me struggle to get in the office and my house without getting up to help me. And there you were—a total stranger, the first time you saw me, you rushed forward to help me. Do you realize you could have tripped and broken your shoulders or something else?"*

He offered me a cup of coffee and continued. *"Good people don't know how good they are nor realize when they've done good deeds. And that's why good men are hard to come by. You're a good man,"* he said. *"Let me show you a house. If you like it, it's yours,"* he offered magnanimously.

"I just got out of college. I can't afford a house yet," I said,

justifiably hesitant.

"*Let's look at it first, OK?*" he said.

So we drove to 25 Wilmington Street, and there he sat down. Construction workers were still remodeling the off-white fenced-in house.

"*Take your time. Go from the basement to the third floor. All the doors are open. Tell me what you think of the house,*" he said.

"*I like the house,*" I said after taking the grand tour.

"*The only thing left is the boiler, and that baby is ready to go,*" he said, admiring the house.

Still, I was not ready to even begin to think of buying a house. Then he gave me a tutorial on buying and owning a home in the United States. Then came the mind-blowing experience; he gave me a check for seven thousand dollars to deposit in my bank account.

"*Open a separate real-estate account with this check, and keep adding money in it,*" he said. "*The mortgage bank will track that account for six months. That's the law.*"

In the meantime, Mr. Schumer began to draft a bank offer-to-buy letter and demanded my name, social security number, and address, place of work, salary, and date of birth. When he finished, he showed me the offer letter.

"*If the bank approves this letter,*" he said, "*that baby is yours, but you will write a check for me in the same amount for your down payment on the house. Call me in two weeks.*"

Two weeks later, I called Mr. Schumer back to ask about the offer letter.

"*The loan was approved,*" he said. "*We'll wait for the bank to schedule your closing date, and then you'll write me a check for seven thousand dollars as I said before. Congratulations.*"

Now thrust into the real-estate arena, I went on and bought another house, at 202 Pleasant Street, the next street over from my first house, from Mr. Schumer two years later. In essence, I bought my first house without a down payment.

My third experience occurred when my in-law, Tunde, and I were

THE AUDACITY OF DESTINY

surveying the property in East Orange, New Jersey, and chatting about the freaking nature of courier business. Tunde told me about a man in Westfield New Jersey, who was selling his van. *"His son went to college with Chijioke and Eke,"* Tunde said. *"I will find out his number, and you can talk to him."*

The next time I went to work with Tunde, he gave me the man's number, then I went home and called the man up, and told him I was looking for a van and I would like to come over and look at the truck he had for sale. So I arrived at his house the following day, parked my car in front of his house and introduced myself. Then he bent forward, peeked inside my car—Lexus ES300 front and back. Yes, I had trash, packages, envelopes, and delivery confirmation slips all over the messy back seat. Suddenly, his interest changed to preserve the prestige of the Lexus brand.

"Are you doing a delivery job with that beautiful Lexus?" he asked me, looking offended.

"Yes, sir, I have no choice," I said and told him all about the irrecoverable financial and economic crash that forced me to use Lexus to deliver craps.

"Good Lord, that's terrible," he said. *"Come inside the house. What would you like to drink?"*

"That will be Pepsi-Cola," I said.

He popped a can of Pepsi and handed it to me. Then we chatted some more about my professional career and the scam that wrecked my life while I sipped on the Pepsi.

"I am so sorry about what happened to you. Trust me you'll come out of it stronger," Mr. Schumer said kindly.

Then he told me the van's radiator had a problem. *"I will tow it to my mechanic's shop in Elizabeth, and you can pick it up there when the mechanic fixed the radiator,"* he said. *"I will pay the mechanic for the repair."*

"Sir, you haven't told me how much you are asking for the van yet," I reminded him.

"I am not asking you for a jack. I want you to park that Lexus and

use the van for your job," he said.

> **I've come to believe that there's goodness deep in every soul that remains dormant until awakened by incidents, voices, and actions that the soul cannot stand by and ignore.**

At that instant, he gave me the keys for the van and the certificate of title. But before getting in my car, he called me back.

"I have to write down some amount on the title," he said. *"Otherwise the Department of Motor Vehicles will not register the van."*

So he wrote down twenty-five dollars in the purchase price column on the title. Then I went home and called Tunde, and told him about the van.

"That's great, Uncle. Now you can make some money with the van," he said, excited for me.

Three days later, I took a bus to the mechanic's shop and drove the van home.

> **There are moments that I wonder about my life—how friendly, kind, generous, and accommodating—on the job and in relationships, people have been towards me. And I feel a sense of guilt because I do not feel deserving of all their kindness. I also wonder what it is about me that send out 'I-need-you' vibration to people whose warm feelings I've enjoyed.**

Here I am, a young man from the continent of Africa—Nigeria to be exact arriving in the US with no idea as to where I'd live, how I'd pay my tuition fees, and how I'd make a living and yet strangers welcomed me to their homes kindly.

Most notably was Mrs. Terry Zdanauk—a white lady who treated me like one of her own in the community where I was probably the only black man around. Or could be my inner-guide using human beings to

THE AUDACITY OF DESTINY

move my journey along the path it wants.

But for whatever reasons, and for what it's worth in my estimation, I have enjoyed the American generosity—I have had my share of it and I am grateful and appreciative of it.

Chapter 16

THE AUDACITY OF DESTINY

The Monkey Wrench

I felt like a still live fish on ice in a butcher's counter on Friday morning.—On Cats.

~ Bukowski

THE AUDACITY OF DESTINY

I Am Crushed

Think about every single person who has ever harmed you, cheated you, defrauded you, or said unkind things about you. Your experience of them is nothing more than a thought that you carry around with you. These thoughts of resentment, anger, and hatred represent slow, debilitating energies that will disempower you. If you could release them, you would know more peace.

~ Wayne W. Dyer

The Irresistible inner-power comes alive and gets to work with the help of a potent tool—the monkey wrench it uses to destroy everything in its path. It does that when it decides the time is right to force a change and move us to the direction it wants. The first thing it does is to take away what you've got going for you; then it puts you through the meat grinder, spits you out, and leaves you questioning your identity—whether or not you're still your real self.

There I was, a manager at one of the most coveted telecommunication companies in the world, at the top of my game, being groomed for the next position—director. By that time, every telecommunication company was no more than illusory-legal-entity; a false American company whose physical presence and employees reside in foreign lands leaving Americans to languish in despair.

The moment I lost my job was the place and time when my rise in the world of high tech stalled and the unwinding of my life and achievements began. So everything changed after being laid off. Fear, self-doubt, and despair set in, as such, was the man, psychologist's perfect stereotype of a low-self-esteem syndrome.

> **Finding a job in an economic recession is difficult. Mildly speaking, job seekers consider it a paragon of achievement.**

To make matters worse, I was in the high echelon of middle management and wage earners. I had looked for jobs until I gave up—realizing there was no job out there for me. And I had collected unemployment checks until my benefit ran out. Things did not seem hopeless to me at first. There's this company called Joe's Enterprise that pitched Kirby vacuum cleaner to homeowners and renters—who're suckers for high-class recognition.

Often in life, the will to survive torques the mind. So I took a sales job there, learned marketing cliché, and drove around New Jersey pitching Kirby, wasting my gas money and dry-cleaning stranger's rugs. During this job, I'd finish my presentation, do the cleaning demonstration, and jump right into the closing session and end up falling flat on my face. It was apparent I was not cut out to be a salesman—I did not have what it takes to be one. To be blunt, I sucked at it.

However, Selling Kirby was a big deal. It was not something at which I should have failed. But it did not matter how artfully or forcefully I managed to deliver the winning phrases—cliché drilled into us during our training session (*"Tell customers you are not selling a vacuum cleaner. Tell them it's Kirby—the dust eater', 'dirt cop', and 'health guard' that will keep your home free of germs"*). Still, the potential clients would not fall for it.

The world was still intact, and I was still alive, although I could not sell Kirby to save my financial decline, which was more like an economic catastrophe. So I took another job, which was a bit different from the previous ones. I chose to go in as fire prevention products manager-in-training.

At this job, I'd produce a certain amount of money in direct sales, pitch the products for package order of predetermined amount, and then I'd make two thousand dollars down payment to open my store.

The first lesson I learned was: *"Convince your family you need their help. [Tell them you'd own your own business and your financial success is guaranteed. Show them the list of people who started the same way you are and became millionaires.]"*

If I had sucked at selling Kirby because of my timidity and my inability to deceive people, here my disdain for lying made, the selling fire prevention products a challenge. It was a monumental task—a grand scheme that schemers sucked me into the second time. Indeed, I had become vulnerable and gullible.

Nevertheless, I pitched to my nephew, Chima and my brother-in-law, Tunde, and a friend, Innocent Okoronkwo, and they bought a package each. I knew they bought their boxes out of pity, but self-preservation would not allow me to think much about it.

I did everything, raised the amount required to get my own office, and again, the company shut down and left the great state of New Jersey.

The Beginning of a Nightmare

I came out of the bank one morning. Around me, people were pounding the pavement busily and with an air of confidence and permanence while for me, the reality was the world crumbling before my eyes. They seemed to breathe in and freely while I was suffocating and sinking fast into an abyss of despair—hardly breathing. I roamed around for a while without feeling the ground I walked on. The day hung around longer than ever as the sun refused to set, and nature showed no mercy to me either. As for sleep, it was no longer a part of the present way I lived but buried in my memory treasure trash-can.

A few days later, my brother-in-law, Tunde, informed me of his lay off, too. So we lamented the state of the economy. *"Have you drafted your résumé?"* I inquired. *"Don't worry, Uncle,"* he said. *"I will start a business and make money with my pen and pencil."*

Not long after that, he started an engineering company, which he named BABS Engineering. Now and then, he called me up to work with him, and he'd pay me for my time. Meanwhile, I had received an eviction notice, so I moved my belongings to storage space and moved in with my girlfriend Renee in Newark, New Jersey, and my nephew moved in with his friends.

As if I hadn't had enough, the storage company evicted me, too. So I moved my stuff to Tunde's house. His new business had begun to take shape. So my worries about him and his wife, my niece, Grace, had subsided substantially.

One day, he invited me to work with him. So we drove to Plainfield, New Jersey and passed our destination. Then we drove around the block a couple of times before we found the address, and then we began to take measurements.

I'd hold one end of the tape while he rolled it out and recorded the lengths. Occasionally he would tell me where to start and stop. It went something like this:

"Uncle, we will measure from the end of the street," he'd say. "Go down. I will tell you when to stop. Keep going. A little bit. Right there."

We finished that job in two hours and went to Edison Industrial Park to look for some equipment he needed for his business. Then we left Edison and went to West New York for another job. Seconds after we'd begun to survey the plot, a sweet aroma permeated the air. I ignored it at first, but gradually, the sweet head-turning-mouth-watering smell overpowered my self-control.

So I felt as though I had to have whatever it was, but I had no money, so I settled for the sweet aroma wafting in my direction and up my nose, distracting me to no end. It seemed to be the only sensible alternative since I could not afford to buy it. I looked around and saw smoke rising out of one tall chimney, clouding the sky. Tunde must have noticed me looking in that direction. I know this because he told me immediately that it was the smell of freshly baked bread. *"It is making me hungry, too,"* he said. *"We will get some when we finish up work."*

We completed the job a few hours later, packed our tools, and went

THE AUDACITY OF DESTINY

to the bakery. There, Tunde picked the loaves he liked. And then he paid for mine too. When we got to his house, my niece Grace had cooked rice and chunky-meaty-sauce; so we ate and relaxed for a while. Before I left, Tunde paid me for the day and urged me to call him whenever my courier master gave me the round-around.

A few weeks later, I started working for Priority, a courier company, located in the industrial park in Edison, New Jersey. My job was to deliver pharmaceutical products to nursing and private homes. It was a sobering experience to see people of all ages on continuous medication, looking as if the world had left them behind and surged ahead.

I was unable to continue to tell the dying that they'd be OK while I could see their health deteriorating daily. I felt as though I was contributing to the sick people's demise by delivering drugs to them; therefore, I quit and joined PDX. Here, my job was to deliver auto parts for Toyota of Morristown. At that moment, I had begun to make money with my van but spent every penny repairing it.

Moment to Remember

How would you know that the current course of your life journey is over and your inner-guide is about to take you in a different direction? Would you even know that everything is about to change?

Aside from not making money delivering auto parts as a freelancing messenger, my van had been in the repair shop for the broken rear axle. So I did not make a nickel for four weeks and did not have the money to pay the mechanic for the repair. In other words, I was unemployed and broke—damn broke!

In the early morning hours of one particular summer day, my clock alarm went off—although I had nowhere to go, setting the alarm and waking up early, was just a habit of mine by which I had lived for long. So I turned over and kicked the alarm clock off the nightstand. The sun

Chuks I. Ndukwe

was already out, and I could see the light filtering through my faux-wood horizontal blinds. I curled up and covered myself again. The alarm promptly went off one more time and then I kicked the shit out of it—down to the floor. It went off again, and then I got up, feeling weird.

For no apparent reason, I began to think about the times when I was still living with my family, with my wife and three daughters; the time I was a manager at Lucent Technologies, designing Internet gateways. I thought of how good life was back then—when I had two houses and money. It was strange because right in those memories was the proof of my ardent loathness towards cash, although I used to make quite a bit of it at the time.

Suddenly I was gripped by a disabling fear—the kind you feel when thick dark clouds cover the sky, high winds force trees to dance to their breaking point, houses shake, and debris pound doors, windows, and roofs with rocket-like power. It was an eerie feeling.

However, when I opened the window, everything was calm. Then after breakfast, I went out to look for a day job—manual labor to ensure that I had some money in my pocket and to avoid the boredom from staying idle at home.

For the most part, I was sitting around, waiting for the mechanic to repair my van—wondering how I'd pay for the repair, and whether I would ever find an engineering job again after failing for six years. By my account, delivering auto parts and pharmaceutical products and making no money did not qualify as employment.

Outright broke and unemployed, and having lost everything I owned when the franchise I bought turned out to be a scam. I had a little to look forward to doing. Still, I persevered and sought comfort in my faith.

Then came an unforgettable day in 2007. On my way home in the evening of that day after traversing the four corners of Newark looking for manual labor.—quite A travail. I stopped by the gas station by my apartment building to buy a pack of peanuts. I stood before the cashier and put the bag of peanut on the counter, and then came the shocker—with my wallet wide open and empty and one hand inside my pocket, I found no money, not even a penny in my pocket to pay for it. So I put the pack of peanut back on the rack.

Still mildly hopeful, I went home, checked my pantry; I had no food to cook. I searched my apartment, desperately looking for some money that I might have carelessly misplaced at some time in the past. I unfolded all my pant pockets inside out, and not even a dime dropped out.

As hope gave way to dismay, I lay down flat on my back that Friday evening and stared at the ceiling. I was hungry, but now, the intense feeling of despair drowned out my appetite for food. A headache pounded my head, and I felt my head burning to a boiling point.

For one thing, I had prayed for a job since I was laid off from my job in 2001—where I was an engineering manager at Lucent Technologies, in New Jersey. Worst yet, at that moment, I was holding an eviction notice in my hand and hours from knocking at the door of a homeless shelter to ask for a bed.

There are moments in life when a son steps up to his father to demand answers—this was one of those moments for me—my father-why-have-you-forsaken-me moment. So I became irate and not in the mood for praying. Why? You may ask. Because all my life, I had believed that I have a special relationship with God. And now it was time to find out why he was not taking our relationship as seriously as I do even though I've tried to act in ways that would receive his approval.

Yes, I had done my very best to keep my end of the deal while all I got from him in response was indifference and punishment. I know he did not create a coward in me, so I summoned the courage and decided to confront him. Then I wondered whether divorcing my wife was such a heinous sin as to deserve the punishing I was getting even though, first, I did not marry in the church; second, she committed adultery and had a baby outside wedlock; worst yet, she had been too arrogant to admit she did even when I found out and asked her. And I remembered I had not just asked, I had begged her to talk about the baby for five years. So I thought, *"How could he be punishing me when all I did was*

Chuks I. Ndukwe

save my poor soul from emotional abuse and spare her the contentious marriage and stressful life?"

Meanwhile, I remembered the advice in Matthew 7:7: "Ask and it shall be given you; seek and you shall find." So, strengthened by the courage and my faith that my pain was deep enough to earn me God's gracious sympathy, I reached out; I asked for three things namely money, a good job—fast, and the affirmation that he was not punishing me for divorcing my estranged wife. Losing my family was killing me. Finally, I said, *"affirmation in the form of the unusual or miraculous event will be welcome."*

As in every storm, fear gave way to a fight for survival. So I felt I had not fought hard enough. *"He has to hear me. I want answers, and I need to know that he heard me,"* I thought.

Then I remembered Matthew 6:33: "But seek first the kingdom of God and his righteousness, and all these things shall be added unto you." *"Why is it that I keep losing instead of having all these things added unto me?"* I thought.

Meanwhile, I hit my bed and hurt my wrist; I kicked the bed frame and ripped off my toenail.

"This can't be happening," I mumbled.

Then the next object I reached for was my pillow. I punched it; I hit it again and knocked it repeatedly until feathers flew all over the bedroom. When I finished cleaning my bedroom, I put a bandage on my toe. Then I turned the light off—only to turn it on again, opened my Bible to John 1:12, and read "As many as receive him, to them gave he the right to become the children of God, even to them that believe in his name."

Then after reminding God that I named myself Chuks [Chukudi] which means I believe in God at the age of thirteen to profess my faith in him, I poured my heart out and questioned the essence of that virtuous living my mom had taught me as well as the value of trust.

THE AUDACITY OF DESTINY

If the faithful cannot be spared homelessness in moments like mine, then what is the use?

Now I've done all the asking: for money, job, and assurance that God was not punishing me for divorcing my estranged wife. So then, I pledged to make this magic moment an original covenant with God. I vowed that if he gave me money, I'd not take part in any social event but instead I will keep to myself until someone invites to a happy occasion that will put a smile on my face. If he gave me a job, to not miss a day until I retired in 2015. But if He affirmed that he was not punishing me for divorcing my estranged wife by sending me my former girlfriend, Melba who I had not seen nor talked to in over a decade—I will quit the job in honor of his grace.

At that point, I lay down on the floor, and suddenly fell asleep and began to dream. It was a strange dream. The child; me was running around, playing in the sand with my cousin Egbichi, chasing after my uncles, and grabbing their hands to lead them into Dad's house. My teachers, people I had met, places I had been, and all my accomplishments and failures were a part of that dream. It was the minutest recount of my childhood and adulthood memories that I had forgotten until that very moment. And when they came back to me in that dream, they ended up illuminating the darkest moment of my life.

I woke up at five-thirty with a knot in my stomach—hunger pangs from not eating the night before. So I lay back on my stomach to sleep away the pain, but it would not go away. In that instant, I remembered Data-Com, a company in Flanders, New Jersey. I drove past every day and never bothered to stop and ask for a job. So I felt I had to go there and ask for employment. Problem being I had no means of getting there. My van was in the shop, and my car had been sitting in the parking lot for a year, and I had not even turned it on once, let alone driven it.

Chuks I. Ndukwe

The Irresistible Inner-Power at Work

At five forty-five in the morning, I hurried out of my apartment through the back door to the parking lot to check on my car. Right there in the parking lot, just outside the back door of the apartment building, lay a silent utility hole—reminding renters that beneath the large building was another structure which was an entangled cobweb of electric wires that PSE&G workers go inside regularly to do their job.

Upon opening the door, there it was: a ten-dollar bill on top of that utility hole which was an *"Aha!"* moment I never knew would come to me. So I picked the dollar note up and walked to my car. The battery was dead, the tires had collapsed to the ground, and the leather seats had cracked—all of them. It was not drivable.

On Monday morning, I called my nephew, Emmanuel, to ask him to give me a ride to Data-Com and wait in his car in the parking lot while I dropped off my résumé.

"I will drop off the résumé. It will take a second," I said. Then I went straight to the HR manager's office and knocked on the door.

"Come in," she said.

I walked into the office and gave her my résumé.

"Chuks, did I pronounce it right?" she asked. *"Sit down and let me see whether Lou is in yet. He came back from a business trip late last night."*

Minutes later, the director, Lou, walked in. We chatted about the economic crash of 2001 along the hallway. Then we got to his office, sat down, and talked some more. Then he told me he did not have any openings. But surprisingly, he told me he could squeeze me into the existing shift structure and asked me my preference.

"I would like to work the weekend shift, from eleven AM on Saturdays to midnight on Sundays," I said.

"Done. Fill out the employment application and the W-9 forms, and come to work on Saturday," he said.

Finally, I ran down the stairs to the parking lot, apologized to Emmanuel for staying too long in the office, and told him, *"I got the job."*

Chapter 17

THE AUDACITY OF DESTINY

The Ultimate Goal

If the leader is filled with high ambition and if he pursues his aims with audacity and strength of will, he will reach them in spite of all obstacles.

~ Carl von Clausewitz

Chuks I. Ndukwe

Destiny

There are no wrong turnings. Only paths we had not known we were meant to walk.

~ Guy Gavriel Kay

The Irresistible inner-power conjures up different images depending upon where you stand in life. In my case, the apt metaphor is the scary, loving uncle who takes you places, lets you enjoy yourself and have the most fun; he tells you time is up and takes you to a different place—not necessarily where you would like to be but where he thinks you need to be.

That is what it does to you. That is what it did to me! I had lost my family, my job and life savings down to the last penny and the franchise I bought turned out to be a scam—it was a complete and utter disaster—the end of my old life.

With unquestionable faith, I asked God for help and the assurance that I was not being punished for divorcing my wife and pledged to things I would or would not do if he granted me the relief I asked. Then two hours and a half later, I found a ten-dollar bill on the cover of a utility hole, and one week later, I found a job, which was the answer to my pleading.

Yet I lost everything I owned and my brother. I survived a near-death incident. And God gave me the assurance I had asked for and I kept my pledge. This assurance came through the visit of a former girlfriend. And then I resumed my normal social life—I had pledged to stay out of until God answered my prayer.

THE AUDACITY OF DESTINY

This narrative is compelling and captivating not only because it's the story of one man who rose from poverty—someone nobody expected to succeed but who still rose from the bottom to reach the zenith, and crashed down to nadir, and got up again. It is a compelling tale because it is a perfect blueprint of the universal journey of life—full of obstacles, wavy, full of twists and turns, ups and downs, and trials and tribulations. It is a book for everybody to read.

For the most part, it feels like a movie sometimes in which I'm the actor. But it's not a movie. I know I would suck at it if it was a movie and I had to act it out. Still, I wonder and ponder over what it all means. I wonder if I'm at the final stop of the journey. I think about what I would do for the rest of my life—what I have left to do. And here's the thing:

I never plan anything—personal. Because nothing I plan ever works. I do things that come to my mind—usually in bed at night and occasionally from people's persuasions. I'm just another toy in my inner guide's playpen.

Now I am back on my feet. My mind had followed it up by purging the pain from the chaos and completely forgetting the agony I had suffered. That's the way it was. This is the way it is. And the way it will always be. Memory keeps memorable and blurs the ugly. Then my nephew, Chima called me one evening and told me Uncle Dr. Kalu Maduka had asked about me. *"He wants you to call him,"* he said.

There could not have been a more persuasive messenger. Uncle Maduka is a highly respected scholar I adored growing up. I had shared some exciting news with him in the past about personal achievements—the day I joined Lucent Technologies and the day Al promoted me to a manager. And I had expressed my concerns about my fear of not meeting the company's expectations. *"Don't worry, you will be fine,"* he had said calmly.

So I called him up. After we'd exchanged the usual pleasantries that are necessary after not having talked for long, then he told me he'd heard I'm back on my feet.

Chuks I. Ndukwe

"I'd been waiting for this news," he said. *"Believe it or not, I knew you'd bounce back because I have monitored your life from childhood, and it's been amazing. I hope you would reach out and teach our young people how to be successful."*

I questioned whether I deserved his compliments, and I also doubted my capacity to teach young people how to be successful after everything I'd experienced—I mean, my failures. I suddenly had a flashback; it was a replay of that dream I'd had which made me wonder, yet again, what it all meant. But then I realized that hidden in the obscurity of that dream was the same message that Uncle Dr. Maduka had just delivered. Still, I kept asking myself, *"What next?"*

Then the answer came one day while I was sharing this narrative with a friend, Ted Haiwata. He was captivated by the twists and turns, the flow from one event to another, and the fantastic connectivity of events that made up my life. *"You must write about it,"* he said, adding reinforcement to Uncle Dr. Maduka's advice. *"You must be kidding,"* I replied. *"Who am I to write my autobiography that people would want to read?"*

I had always thought of writing as a skill that was carved out for a select few who had the unique gift of poetry, literary artistry, and rigor—the unique ability to stitch words together and breathe life into them. In my eyes, I am not one of those people.

> **One thing to be said about living a long, active life; you acquire experience and live out your principle like one I've often temperately articulated; that experience is not what you have seen, done, or touched but what you do with it.**

Therefore, I borrowed from my experience. I had been afraid when I got my first job, terrified when I got the second job and scared when I got my last post. And fear had always propelled me to exceed expected high performances, so why should it be any different this time? As with everything, I have done every time I took a scary position; I'd draft a

THE AUDACITY OF DESTINY

mission statement. So before writing the first word, I wrote my mission statement.

> **I will strive to do my best and to write about my life experiences to inspire, uplift the spirit, and seek to make a difference in the lives of my readers.**

As I began to write, I gained a greater appreciation for the audacity of destiny. I have also had a personal experience of the tremendous pain the pursuit of it can inflict on a person, and how it could infuse the mind with the precious memory and images from which to draw. I have come to realize that when you are at the place you need to be, the only thing left is to tell the story. The only thing to do is to share the memory with the hope that the telling helps somebody.

> **After all, what is the use of telling a story if there is nothing to learn from it?**

This telling provides a unique window into the blurred mechanics and nature of the human interiority complex—the power that leads the journey towards destiny.

Moment of Reflection

The lesson I learned about fear each time I get into a new position is that I was paying my dues to guilt—the guilt of possible failure to meet or exceed the expected high performance. But it turned out in each case, I thrived and exceeded the expectations I feared I would not attend.

There had been moments I'd sat back and wondered: What I would have been if I didn't like school and learning growing up, would I have made it through primary school? What if my teachers didn't love me as much as they did, could I have had an interest in school? What if that American scientist, Mr. Marshal, hadn't demonstrated electric light in my classroom, what alternative interest would I have had? What if I hadn't volunteered to repair a burnt system at TeleAudit while still in college, would I have made it to Spectrametrics? What if I did not

Chuks I. Ndukwe

volunteer to redesign AT&T telephone interface at Codex Corporation, would I have pioneered the caller-Id technology and would the launching of my career been as exciting as it was?

Each time that I grappled with these questions, I would end up at the same place with conflicting and endless thoughts each falling short in clarity and certainty, but the truth is that; *"I can't imagine what the answer would have been."*

Epilogue

I live for coincidences. They briefly give to me the illusion or the hope that there's a pattern to my life, and if there's a pattern, then maybe I'm moving toward some kind of destiny where it's all explained.

~ Jonathan Ames

This telling is of my journey of life. For the most part, the mission is for the pursuit of happiness or better yet a journey in search of my reason for being—my destiny. However, when viewed through the narrow lenses of the written work or categories of literary genre, it is my autobiography. But as the title suggests, it's more than that. It is a reflection on the journey when our inner-power is leading the way. It is also about the battles lost, and the contests won, the immense pain and suffering the journey can inflict on us, and how our inner-power in concert with our quest for destiny can shatter all obstacles along the way and lead us forward to the future. To that end, this telling is merely anecdotal to the journey of life in general—it's everybody's story.

To be sure, one universal aspect of the journey that will forever remain constant is its beginning—birth, although the preparation varies in some ways depending on where the tour starts. For me, the love of my family was the backdrop that remains a formidable foundation of my life and reminds me never to stop to remember how I got here.

The takeaway of this telling is significant, and I did not realize it until I read it back to myself. That is that each inspiring narrow band of light in the telling—overcoming an obstacle, dark, frightening moments, and tragic failures not only holds its unique meaning but also the lesson that helps me put every mile, every signpost, every turn, and every minute of the journey in perspective.

Another thing that grabbed me is that I am in many ways a little baton in a yet to be defined relay race—in this journey that each runner hands off carefully and safely to the next—along the race track to the finish line where I wonder what the cross-line would be.

Lest you spread me out on the butcher block of the untalented to rip me apart, I've not stepped out to showcase talent, poetry, or literary artistry and rigor. What I've strived to do is tell a story of an imperfect life that had no chance at the beginning but who made it by the sheer audacity of destiny and the kindness of total strangers to bring you this story despite all the overwhelming social and economic obstacles.

A point often overlooked is the invisible machinery of human being, which this telling brings into focus and defines as *'interiority complex'* for lack of a better term. This mythical interiority complex comprises of the following: (awesome Irresistible inner-power—the guide). (Conscience—that decides between right and wrong). (Non-carnal senses—that see beyond the bright light of the day and darkness of night to preview events that are yet to unfold), and (the inner-voice—that counsel us on the laws of nature), on what is right, and what is wrong. It keeps us moving along within the guardrails of the natural order.

Without a doubt, life is a journey; an arduous journey, indeed. It starts from the day we are born and takes us in different directions—across the valleys, up the mountains, overland, air, and sea. We go to places where we meet different people and of different nationalities, learn different lessons, acquire various skills, and play different games on the different stages—at the different theaters of life.

But it's during the waning days when we find ourselves on the Broadway-theater of life. The stage is where we get to perform our final act and where the magic happens. You look around, and the most massive invisible audience cheers and the inner-power judges every movement you make, every word you say and how you say it. It judges your performance—your work. For it is if and only if your inner-guide matches your act to your reason for being can you honestly proclaim that "yes this is my destiny.

THE AUDACITY OF DESTINY

To some extent, though, destiny is like planting our footsteps deeply and firmly on the sand of time for a man who passes without leaving a trace is one who the world forgets soon after he departs.

Meanwhile, I'm sitting here thinking, "Who am I writing for?" I don't know the answer for sure. However, I can say *everybody with a fair degree of confidence can be a reader of this book and can benefit from it."*

Here are some reasons to read this book; buy one for your kid's birthday, graduation, or wedding present or donate it to someone who's down on his luck and needs the motivation to get up:

- It reminds us that a child's success depends mostly on the discipline and character that his parents instilled in him.

- It reinforces the notion that children do not love school because they're told to but because they find school fun, have friends and are inspired to learn often by their parents' respectful relationships with their teachers and the school.

- It suggests that when parents expose their children to events inside and outside the home or school that capture their imagination—something tangible to think about—then the goal and pursuit of it becomes a mission.

- It casts light on the concept of human interiority complex (Irresistible inner-power—the guide, conscience, non-carnal senses, and the inner-voice) which unify in contingent symbiosis to move the journey along to its destiny.

- It cautions us not to take the easy way out, do the wrong thing, or sell your souls to recover from adversity but to do the right thing no matter how gruelingly long time it takes to recover. Because it's the ultimate choice, we make that defines success or failure.

At this moment in time, I am reviewing life from a place in my soul—a site free from the blurriness of vision and obscurity of memory; where everything has meaning and every event has context. I'm writing to unveil the mystery of human interiority complex and to add clarity to the mythology of destiny and say to young people today and those yet unborn; Sure! You can become or achieve whatever inspires or grabs your imagination. First, you must audibly articulate your wish and pursue it with thoughtful and persistent action-taking. Say loudly and boldly to your creator, "*This is what I want to be—this is where I want you to take me.*" And go for it for every unarticulated wish is nothing but a wasted thought. Yes! That's how you invite your inner-power to lead the way to destiny.

Let me be candid; it would have been inconceivable that a not-so-bright child like me could be here with a platform to share my story. So I think of life in terms of that metaphorical journey and try to put my ride in context because it represents everybody's journey no matter how poor or how rich. We're never alone on this journey even when it seems as though we are all by ourselves.

Acknowledgements

I want to acknowledge my editors, Irene, Jason, Nicholas, and the entire project team for the fantastic job they have done in shaping this narrative.

About The Author

***

Chuks I. Ndukwe was once a sought after engineer in the High Tech industry. He graduated from Northeastern University in Boston, Massachusetts and worked for such companies as Codex Corporation, USRobotics, ADC Telecom, and Lucent Technologies where he mentored junior engineers and managed research and development departments.

During his career, Ndukwe demonstrated strategic management skills, and his problem-solving skills earned him "Key Contributor Award" at ADC Telecom, Minnetonka Minnesota. He built a strong team of engineers that performed above expectations—designing such technologies as caller identification, modems, routers, and Internet gateways.

Ndukwe is now retired and lives in Newark, New Jersey where he devotes his time writing to inspire others.

Other Books

Like this Book?

If you enjoyed this book, below are other books
by **Chuks I. Ndukwe**

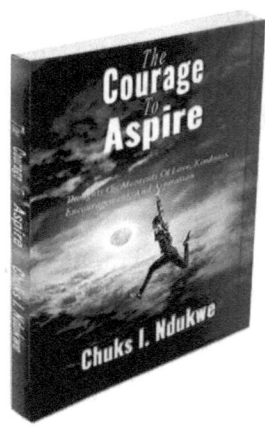 

The Courage To Aspire **A Matter Of Faith**
(Trade Paperback) (Trade Paperback)

Distributed by IngramSpark and Available on Amazon,
ikebiebooks.com, and everywhere books are sold